Britten

Britten

David Matthews

HAUS PUBLISHING · LONDON

First published in Great Britain in 2003 by
Haus Publishing Limited
32 Store Street
London WC1E 7BS

A CIP catalogue record of this work is available from the British Library

ISBN 1-904341-21-7 (paperback)
ISBN 1-904341-39-X (hardback)

Typeset by Lobster Design

Printed and bound by Graphicom in Vicenza, Italy

Cover image: Benjamin Britten, 1956, TopFoto
Back cover: Benjamin Britten, 1970, TopFoto
Page iii: Britten at Crag House, Aldeburgh, early 1950s. Photo: Roland
Haupt. Courtesy of The Britten-Pears Library

Contents

Preface

In 1966 I was working as a freelance music copyist and editor in order to finance my intended life as a composer. One of the people who employed me was Donald Mitchell, who had recently established the firm of Faber Music, primarily in order to publish Britten's latest music. In the spring of 1966, Martin Penny, who was preparing the special 'rehearsal score' of *The Burning Fiery Furnace*, fell ill, and someone was needed in a hurry to complete the score. I was asked, and was able to finish the job in time. I went to the premiere of the new piece at the Aldeburgh Festival, which took place in Orford Church. After the performance I was introduced to Britten, who said kindly *I hope you enjoyed hearing your notes.* Later that year I incorporated Britten's revisions into the score, and since I seemed to have passed the necessary test of competence I became, over the next four years, an occasional assistant to Britten's regular music assistant Rosamund Strode. Among the tasks I was assigned were preparing the rehearsal score of *The Prodigal Son* and the vocal score of *Owen Wingrave*. I also made a fair copy of the full score of *Owen Wingrave*, with help from my brother Colin, who later took over from me for the vocal score of *Death in Venice*. After Britten's heart operation in 1973, I made the vocal score of *Paul Bunyan* and a reduction for two pianos.

From 1967 to 1970 I also helped with the editing of Britten's music and the works he conducted at the Aldeburgh Festival, for instance *Idomeneo*, of which, in the tradition of Mahler and Strauss, he made his own edition. I attended many of his rehearsals. I used to go to Aldeburgh to stay for extended periods, and was assigned an office in the former stable buildings beside the Red House which are now part of the Britten-Pears Library. Most days

Britten would call in to say hello; sometimes I would join him for tea, and on one occasion I had supper with him and we talked at length about the contemporary music scene. I think he felt a little isolated from it but still concerned to keep in touch with what was going on. After supper he played me some gramophone records: Kirsten Flagstad singing Sibelius – I remember his enthusiasm for her voice – and the Indian flautist Pannalal Ghosh, whose playing greatly interested him at that time and influenced some of the melodic writing in *The Prodigal Son*.

I was shy and somewhat in awe of Britten – not surprisingly, as he was the first adult composer I had met – and now feel that I could perhaps have made more use of the opportunities I was given. I could have shown him my music, for instance, but didn't. I was somewhat wary of the Aldeburgh scene, and a little afraid of becoming too closely drawn into it. I was also aware, as everyone was, of Britten's hyper-sensitivity and that one had to be careful not to upset him by venturing any rash opinions. He, I must say, was never anything other than kind, considerate and helpful.

I realize what an extraordinary privilege it was for me to have been an apprentice in his workshop, observing at close hand a great composer solving all the problems of composition and performance in his supremely practical way. It was the best kind of training for a young composer, and this book is in one sense an expression of my gratitude to the man who made it possible.

I should like to thank the staff of the Britten-Pears Library, in particular Nicholas Clark, Elizabeth Gibson and Jennifer Doctor, for their generous help while I was researching the book. I am grateful to the Trustees of the Britten-Pears Foundation and of the Lennox Berkeley Estate for allowing me to quote from copyright material, which is not to be further reproduced without written permission from the Trustees. I owe a great deal to the existing Britten literature, above all to Humphrey Carpenter's full and detailed biography and the two published volumes of Britten's diaries and letters, edited by Donald Mitchell and Philip Reed. The staff at Haus, especially Barbara Schwepcke, were exceptionally understanding and helpful, and Peter Sheppard Skærved's editorial supervision was invaluable. Mark Doran and Jenifer Wakelyn's contributions to the final text as unofficial editors were extraordinarily scrupulous and thorough (Mark Doran also wrote the sidebar on Hans Keller). David Harman, Jean Hasse, Colin Matthews, Donald Mitchell and Norman Worrall also read the text and made extremely helpful comments. In addition Judith Bingham, Jonathan Del Mar and Rosamund Strode supplied valuable details.

DAVID MATTHEWS

Note: Britten's spelling remained somewhat uncertain throughout his life – it was one of those habits that he preserved from his boyhood. As well as spelling mistakes, there are characteristic idiosyncracies such as 'abit'. In the quotations from his letters and diaries, no attempt has been made to correct Britten's text.

A Boy Was Born

Benjamin Britten was born in Suffolk, and lived almost all his life in that most easterly county of England. Few 20th-century artists have remained so closely in touch with their roots as Britten. Staying near to where he was born helped him maintain contact with the childhood world to which he so often returned in his music, and with the sea – a constant stimulus for his life and his work.

The Britten family lived in the fishing port of Lowestoft, in a house overlooking the North Sea. In later life Britten was to make his home in the nearby town of Aldeburgh, where for some years he had a house right on the seafront. Elias Canetti suggested – surely correctly – that the sea is the national symbol for the English, as the forest is for the Germans. The English landscape may have inspired more music, and landscape painting is perhaps our foremost contribution to the visual arts; yet the sea, which offers, in Canetti's words, 'transformation and danger',[1] has a more potent hold on the English imagination. No composer, not even Debussy, has evoked the sea more powerfully than Britten in his opera *Peter Grimes*, the work that made him famous. Britten's first memory, he told his friend and publisher Donald Mitchell, was *the sound of rushing water*[2] as he was being born – but can one possibly remember one's own birth? Might he not have been recalling the sound of the sea, the constant background to his childhood?

His family, Britten said, was *very ordinary middle-class*[3] – a somewhat misleading remark, as there was nothing ordinary about Britten's childhood. His father, Robert, was a dentist with a successful practice, but he disliked his job and if there had

Robert and Edith Britten at the time of their engagement

been enough money in the family he would have become a farmer. He was not musical, and would probably have preferred his son to choose another career than the precarious life of a musician; his wife, however, overruled him. In photographs his hooded eyes make him look a little sinister, though he seems to have been a kindly if strict father, who was known to his children as 'Pop', was fond of whisky, played golf, and liked to go for long walks. Despite his misgivings about his son's fanatical devotion to music, he was proud of him: he clearly recognized that Benjamin was unusual, and he was not unresponsive to his special qualities. In his diary for 18 August 1928, aged 14, Britten wrote: *Daddy remarks, in the evening, that I will be a terrible one for love, and that when the time comes I will think that my love is different from any other and that it is the love.* Britten writes *REMEMBER* alongside this insightful piece of advice. The letters from 'Pop' to Benjamin and his sister Beth, quoted in her book about her brother, are affectionate, if sometimes a little awkwardly expressed.

When Robert Britten was 24 he married Edith Hockey, who was four years older. Hers was the artistic side of the family: her brother Willie became organist of a church in Ipswich and directed the Ipswich Choral Society; another brother was also a church organist, and her sister Queenie was a painter who exhibited at the Royal Academy in London. There were also skeletons in the family cupboard: Edith's father had been born out of wedlock – the family story was that her grandfather had been an aristocrat – and her mother became an alcoholic and spent some of her life in what Beth Britten calls 'a home for inebriates'.[4] Edith was a beautiful woman, as her engagement photograph shows: *such a girl as even I could lose my heart to*,[5] Britten wrote shortly after her death. Music came to play a central role in her life. She was a keen amateur singer, who sang with the Lowestoft Musical Society, for which she acted as Secretary. The choir gave concerts at the Evangelical church which she attended regularly, though her husband did not. She also loved to perform at home, singing songs by Schubert and Roger Quilter among others, with 'Beni' accompanying her. She also played piano duets with him, as she was a capable pianist. Her voice was mezzo-soprano and, as Britten's boyhood friend Basil Reeve noticed (and his sister Beth agreed), uncannily similar in tone to that of Britten's partner in adult life, the tenor Peter Pears.

Ben and Beth with their mother

Edith's fourth and last child, Edward Benjamin (his first name was soon dropped), was born on 22 November 1913, the day consecrated to St Cecilia, patron saint of musicians. He was a lovely boy, with blue eyes and golden curly hair, and he became his mother's favourite. His health was never robust: at the age of three months he almost died of pneumonia, and he had a congenitally weak heart that was ultimately responsible for his premature death. He did not sleep

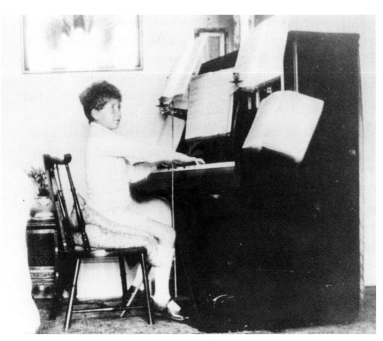

The young genius apparently playing from four scores at once

well, and Edith often had to sing him to sleep. It is almost impossible to exaggerate the importance of this archetypal maternal practice to Britten's psyche and to his later artistic development. In adult life, Britten was never entirely able to trust the outside world. How many of us can, one might ask? Yet Britten's uneasiness was extreme, and his music reveals it: his world is a place of danger and often of terror, where innocence is readily corrupted. There can be temporary reassurance in beauty and in love, but sleep is the only sure place where security and trust may be regained. The image of sleep as a refuge is something that Britten returns to again and again in his music: in the *Serenade*, the *Nocturne*, the *War Requiem*. The idyllically happy ending of *A Midsummer Night's Dream* is possible because the opera *is* a dream.

In all these works it is the singing voice that brings balm, and especially the voice of Peter Pears, who in many ways took on the maternal role in Britten's life after her death.

Edith had been disappointed that her other children, Robert, the eldest of the four, and the two sisters Barbara and Beth, had shown no special aptitude for music, though Robert had learned the violin. Benjamin was different. He started playing the piano, he said, *as soon as I could walk*,[6] and was soon improvising experimentally and trying to write down what he played. His mother helped him to learn the rudiments of piano technique, and at seven he began formal lessons with Miss Ethel Astle, one of the mistresses at his first school. He quickly showed great talent as a pianist, and started to compose in earnest. Edith did all she could to encourage him. Many successful children benefit from an ambitious mother, and few mothers have been so ruthlessly ambitious as Mrs Britten. She completely dominated Benjamin's early life; as Basil Reeve observed, she was '*determined* that he should be a great musician'.[7] She would soon be telling friends that her son would be 'The Fourth B' after Bach, Beethoven and Brahms (and perhaps she was right). Because Britten was the centre of her attention, the object of her most fervent love, he soon came to believe that he was special, someone around whom the world should revolve.

At the age of eight he was sent to a nearby preparatory school, South Lodge, as a day boy. Most of the other pupils were boarders. Britten enjoyed learning mathematics, which was taught by the headmaster, Thomas Sewell, and was enthusiastic about games, especially cricket; but he was shocked by the spectacle of other boys being beaten (he mostly managed to stay out of trouble himself). For his ninth birthday his Uncle Willie gave him Stainer and Barrett's *A Dictionary of Musical Terms*, and soon afterwards his attempts at composing became more sophisticated. Among his first proper compositions was a set of 'Twelve Songs for the Mezzo Soprano and Contralto Voice'; they included a setting of Burns's 'O that I had ne'er been married', and 'Beware' to words by Longfellow. It is a little disconcerting to find the texts of both these songs are warnings against women. 'Beware' was clearly an important song for Britten, since he copied it out a number of times. The two stanzas that Britten set are as follows:

> I know a maiden fair to see,
>   Take care!
> She can both false and friendly be,
>   Beware! Beware!
>   Trust her not,
> She is fooling thee!
>
> She has two eyes, so soft and brown,
>   Take care!
> She gives a side-glance and looks down,
>   Beware! Beware!
>   Trust her not,
> She is fooling thee!

No doubt his mother sang these words with her son at the piano; one wonders what she made of them. They are a telling reflection of the intensity of the mother-son relationship, which must have contained hate as well as love. The avowals of love from Britten's side are plain to see: one of his earliest surviving letters (from November 1923) is signed *With tons and cwts and lbs and ozs of pakages of Love, Your own tiny little (sick-for-Muvver) BENI.*[8] Later letters read even more like those of a lover: *You will come, won't you darling, when the snow has gone and when I am better and allowed to go out with you? Please, please, do!*, Britten pleads in a letter from his public school in February 1929, a letter which is signed *your worshipping, adoring loving (etc) son.*[9] Edith in turn demanded much from her son: a weekly ritual was to play duets every Sunday afternoon on the piano in the upstairs drawing room (the room that Mr Britten called 'Heaven'). There was a specially prescribed piece: the *Siegfried Idyll*, the song of love that Wagner had composed as a present for his wife Cosima shortly after the birth of their son Siegfried. It was re-enacted as a love duet between Britten and his mother. At this time, and for many years afterwards, each of them was the centre of the other's emotional life. It

Leaving for school, 1928

hardly needs to be said that Mrs Britten was powerfully influencing the course of her son's emotional development and very likely his sexuality, although the consequences would not become apparent until much later.

Despite his long school day – from 7.30 in the morning until 8 at night – by the age of 11 Britten was producing enormous quantities of music, at first mostly for piano solo. In 1934 he selected a few of these early pieces and rewrote them for strings to make his *Simple Symphony*, and much later, in 1970, he had 'Five Walztes' published (he preserved the child's spelling). Otherwise, in adult life he was quite nonchalant about his early compositions. These soon became more ambitious: from March 1925 to July 1926 he worked intermittently on a large-scale mass for soloists,

Frank Bridge (1879–1941) began as an English Romantic like his contemporaries Vaughan Williams (1872–1958) and Holst (1874–1934). *The Sea* (1910) is a fine example of this early manner. In the next few years he developed his musical language towards a more progressive style that took into account the harmonic innovations of Debussy, Ravel and Skryabin, and later of Schoenberg, Berg and Bartók. In the mid-1920s probably no English composer was as alive as Bridge to the latest continental developments, and Britten's progressive stance as a teenager was almost entirely due to Bridge's influence. Besides *Enter Spring*, his major mature works include *Oration* (1930) for cello and orchestra – a passionate protest on behalf of the dead of the First World War – and the Third and Fourth String Quartets. Bridge was also a fine viola player and an accomplished conductor.

chorus (often in eight parts) and an accompaniment which at first is a piano reduction but by the Credo has become a short score with instrumental indications. The Mass fills four notebooks: at the end of the fourth – in the middle of the Credo – it suddenly stops. The skilful choral writing had resulted from hearing his mother's choir and studying vocal scores of pieces she was singing, such as Handel's *Messiah* or Stainer's *Crucifixion*; his knowledge of the repertoire at this time was almost entirely derived from scores he saw and played through, as there was no gramophone or wireless in the house. He had, however, also begun viola lessons in 1923 with Audrey Alston, a friend of Mrs Britten. Mrs Alston played in a string quartet in Norwich; Britten went to some of their concerts and on 30 October 1924 he attended his first orchestral concert, at the Norwich Triennial Festival, where he heard a piece by a living British composer, Frank Bridge's *The Sea*, and in his own words he was *knocked sideways*.[10] It is telling that it should have been a work inspired by the sea that so affected him; and interesting to note that three of Britten's *Four Sea Interludes* in *Peter Grimes* correspond to movements in Bridge's work. This opens with a depiction of a calm sea, with evocative phrases on violins, woodwind and harp, like Britten's 'Dawn'; its third movement is called 'Moonlight' and the finale is an evocation of a storm.

The next Triennial Festival, in 1927, was the occasion for the premiere of Bridge's orchestral masterpiece *Enter Spring*. Britten was again present, and he was introduced to Bridge, who was staying with the Alstons. Bridge had only to talk to Britten for a few minutes before he realized that the boy was quite exceptional. Britten showed him some of his music and Bridge, greatly impressed, suggested that he should come to London during his school holidays for composition lessons with him, and for piano lessons with his friend Harold Samuel, who taught at the Royal College of Music. Despite some opposition from Britten's parents – his father in particular was suspicious of Bridge's flamboyant personality – it was agreed that Britten would begin lessons in the Christmas holidays. So began one of the classic musical apprenticeships, and a deep friendship that continued until Bridge's death in 1941. He and his wife Ethel had no children, and Britten soon became a substitute son for them. Bridge's letters, witty and wise, testify to the warmth of the relationship. Britten's side of the correspondence is unfortunately lost. Bridge was a demanding teacher: his lessons were long and, as Britten recalled, *often I used to end these marathons in tears; not that he was beastly to me, but the concentrated strain was too much for me.*[11] Bridge's method was to *play every passage slowly on the piano and say, 'Now listen to this – is this what you meant?'. . . And he really taught me to take as much trouble as I possibly could over every passage, over every progression, over every line.*[12]

Britten's studies with Bridge soon bore fruit. Although Beethoven and Brahms were to remain his chief musical gods throughout his teenage years (and Beethoven well into his twenties), the 14-year-old, encouraged by his teacher, was now getting to know the music of contemporary composers and beginning to explore a more advanced musical idiom. In the past two years he had been writing orchestral music in earnest: between April 1926 and the time he met Bridge he had composed two large-scale overtures, five *Poèmes*, a *Suite fantastique* for piano and orchestra, a Symphony in D minor for huge orchestra including eight horns and oboe d'amore (117 pages of full score in five weeks of term-time at South Lodge, during which he also composed two of the *Poèmes*!) and a big Lisztian symphonic poem, *Chaos and Cosmos*. Two more orchestral pieces were composed in the first months of 1928, and show the influence of Bridge's orchestral writing.

None of these works, however, is quite as remarkable as the *Quatre chansons françaises* he wrote in the summer of 1928 as a wedding anniversary present for his parents. Romantic world-weariness, a common enough symptom of adolescence, is expressed here in a sophisticated and exquisitely imagined way. In April he had heard a recording of Debussy's *L'Après-midi d'un faune* and bought the score of Ravel's *Introduction and Allegro*; his new-found interest in those composers encouraged him to set the French language, which he does with assurance. It also gave him a model for an orchestral sound, though some of his sonorities are also quite original, for instance his use of piano and harp together. The harmony veers off in places towards what sounds like Bergian Expressionism (Bridge probably had a score of *Wozzeck* that Britten had seen). In his setting of Hugo's 'L'enfance', where a mother lies dying while her five-year-old son innocently sings (a very Brittenish subject, though a somewhat morbid one in the context of a piece written for his parents' anniversary), Britten weaves a French nursery rhyme in and out of the texture in a very Debussyan way; the final song, Verlaine's 'Chanson d'Automne', ends with a Tristanesque cadence on the word 'morte' in the *Liebestod*'s closing key of B major (notated by Britten as C flat). Britten owned 13 Wagner miniature scores at this time, and his enthusiasm for Wagner, and for *Tristan* especially, went on for some years. *He is the master of us all*,[13] he wrote in 1933. Was it because he soon outgrew this late-Romanticism that he made no attempt to have these extraordinary songs played during his lifetime? They were not performed until 1980, but they have since taken their place in the repertory as an example of youthful genius almost equal to that of Mozart and Mendelssohn.

Britten's largely happy time at South Lodge School now came to a close. He had ended up as head boy and *Victor Ludorum* (champion at games), though he blotted his copybook by writing an end-of-term essay on 'Animals' which turned into an attack on hunting and went on to condemn all forms of aggression, especially war. The essay was the first statement of his lifelong commitment to pacifism, which had been stimulated by talking to Bridge about the First World War; it shocked his teachers and he received no marks. In September 1928 he became a boarder at a public school about 50 miles from his home, Gresham's School at Holt, in Norfolk, to which he had won a music scholarship. The poets W H Auden and Stephen Spender and the composer Lennox Berkeley had all been pupils there. Gresham's was quite progressive for its day: boys were not forced to join the Officers' Training Corps (and so Britten did not) and the music department was well established, with a school orchestra and regular chamber concerts. In spite of this, Britten was immediately and seriously unhappy. The *swearing and vulgarity*[14] of his fellow pupils disgusted him, and he took a dislike to the music master, Walter Greatorex, who criticized his piano playing and was scornful of his love of Beethoven. Greatorex little realized what heresy he was committing. This was the boy who after listening to the Kreisler recording of the Violin Concerto had written in his diary: *Oh! Beethoven, thou art immortal; has anything ever been written like the pathos of the 1st & 2nd movements, and the joy of the last?*,[15] and for whom the gift from his parents of the full score of *Fidelio* on his 16th birthday was a *red letter day*[16] in his life. Britten in turn was highly critical of Greatorex. His diary, which he had begun at the beginning of 1928 and which he continued with daily entries for the next nine years, contains a number of caustic comments about him: *how ever the man got the job here I cannot imagine. His idea of rhythm, logic, tone, or the music is absolutely lacking in sanity.*[17] (It is worth noting that this was a view markedly different to that of both Spender and Auden: the latter thought he was a musician 'of the first rank'[18] and compared his playing of Bach on the organ to Albert Schweitzer.) Greatorex's attitude was no doubt influenced by his resentment that Britten was going elsewhere for piano and composition lessons; what is more the precocious confidence of Britten's musical opinions must have been a threat to his authority.

Britten longed for home and for the beloved mother who had sent him away. It is now that his letters to her rise to a new pitch of intimacy and painful intensity. His diary too – which until its last few years is mostly an unemotional record of things done –

On the sea front at Lowestoft, c.1928–9

underlines his loneliness. Shortly after the start of the new term in January 1929, he became ill with 'flu and spent much of the term in the sickroom. He was finally sent home to recuperate, and the day after returning to school he recorded: *I spend probably one of the most miserable days in all my life. Lying in bed in the dormetry, feeling absolutely rotten. Yearning for home and everybody there. Am sick once in morning. Why <u>did</u> they send me back, to go to bed directly?*[19] It is hard not to draw the conclusion that the prolongation of his illness was to a certain extent psychologically motivated. By remaining ill he could be certain of attracting the care and attention he sought. And he could read books as well as write music: bed was a favourite place to work. During this particular illness, he read Elizabeth von Arnim's *Caravaners*, Victor Hugo's *The Toilers of the Sea* and Scott's *Rob Roy.* He composed a Rhapsody for string quartet, his most 'advanced' piece to date, which caused him much trouble. His music was now similar in style to the chamber pieces that Frank Bridge was writing, such as the Third String Quartet and the Rhapsody Trio for two violins and viola – a work that much later, in 1966, Britten was responsible for seeing into print.

More chamber works followed, each more radical than its predecessor. Several of these pieces were for Britten to play during the holidays with his friends Basil Reeve (piano) and Charles Coleman (violin). The Two Pieces for violin, viola and piano, composed in November and December 1929, are atonal in places. In his diary for 20 November he wrote: *I am thinking much about modernism in art. Debating whether Impressionism, Expressionism, Classicism etc. are right. I have half decided on Schönberg. I adore Picasso's pictures.*[20] A few months later, hearing a *marvellous Schönberg concert*[21] on the radio, which included a performance of *Pierrot lunaire*, he is more positive about the controversial composer. It was just at this time (April 1930) that he was writing his *Quartettino* for string quartet, which marked almost the furthest point he reached, though it is still centred on C sharp, the note on which it begins and ends. His later music would sometimes employ both a high level of dissonance and a blurring of tonality (for instance the grinding climax of the first movement of the *Spring Symphony*, or the first movement of the Third Quartet) but, with one small exception, no complete piece would ever be so thoroughly chromatic as this. Schoenbergian modernism, the language of an isolated and anguished prophet, was for a while an appealing path for the ultra-sensitive, lonely schoolboy, conscious of the superiority of his taste and abilities to those of his so-called elders and betters.

He was not using this highly chromatic language exclusively. At the same time as these experimental pieces, he wrote a *Hymn to the Virgin* for unaccompanied chorus which is more characteristic of his mature style. He composed it in a few hours while recovering from another bout of illness, and it was one of the pieces accepted by his first publisher, Oxford University Press. Nor should his two years at Gresham's be seen in an entirely negative light. His school friend David Layton remembers him as being much happier than his diary would suggest, and an enthusiastic participator in school games.[22] In his second year Britten took a more active part in the school's musical life, playing the viola in Saturday chamber music concerts, giving solo piano recitals to great acclaim; finally having one of his more adventurous pieces played in public, a Bagatelle for violin, viola and piano, with Britten playing the viola and Greatorex, no less, the piano. These concerts, however, were no substitute for the chamber music he played in his holidays with Basil Reeve and Charles Coleman, and home was still the refuge he longed for. Britten was due to take his School Certificate at the end of his sixth term, and it was clear to him that after this he could stand no more of Gresham's.[23]

A way out presented itself: in May 1930 the Royal College of Music in London offered a music scholarship and Britten entered for it. He sent a portfolio of recent compositions, including two

From The Musical Times, May 1929:

SIR, – The other day, when playing Beethoven's C major Sonata for 'cello and pianoforte, Op. 102, No. 1, I noticed a great similarity between a theme which appears in the Finale several times:

and the last line of Davy's song, 'The Bay of Biscay'.

I have never read anything about this in any book on Beethoven, and I wonder if any reader has. I suppose it is not possible that Beethoven could have known the song; and I should be grateful if a reader could inform me as to the date of it.

May I add how I wish that there could be more performances of this beautiful Sonata by first-rate artists; as far as I know there is not even a gramophone record of it. – Yours, & c.,

E. BENJAMIN BRITTEN
21, Kirkley Cliff Road, Lowestoft.

. . . which received this reply in the June issue:

SIR, – In reply to Mr Britten's letter in your May issue, I think it extremely probable that Beethoven was acquainted with Davy's song 'The Bay of Biscay', for Davy's songs and incidental music to the plays of his period had an enormous vogue, if we can trust reference books. Moreover, we know that Beethoven took great interest in the wars of his time.

Davy was a contemporary of his, being born at Exeter, December 23, 1763, and dying in extreme poverty in St Martin's Lane, London, February 22, 1824. – Yours, & c.,

REGINALD SILVER
Micro Cottage, Colyton, Devon.

vocal works which were later published: a song, 'The Birds', to words by Hilaire Belloc, and *A Wealden Trio* for female voices, a setting of a poem by Ford Madox Ford. After an anxious few weeks of waiting, he was asked to come to London for an examination. He found the written examination in compositional techniques very easy, and was interviewed in the afternoon by Ralph Vaughan Williams, John Ireland, and a harmony and counterpoint teacher, Sydney Waddington, who according to Ireland thought it wasn't 'decent'[24] that an English public schoolboy should be writing music like this – a remark that foreshadows much of the criticism of Britten that was to come. They nevertheless awarded him the scholarship, somewhat to Britten's surprise. A few weeks later he left school, having passed his Certificate and collected a number of prize books that he had chosen himself, including scores of Strauss's *Don Quixote* and Schoenberg's *Pierrot lunaire*. Perhaps he finally realized that a school that raised no objections to his choice of the latter wasn't such a bad place after all. His diary records: *I am terribly sorry to leave such boys as these*[25] . . . *I didn't think I should be so sorry to leave.*[26] And yet, the day after he arrived home, he was to write the *ne plus ultra* of his modernist pieces, a short, untitled *not-too-nice piece for Viola Solo*[27] (it has now been published as *Elegy*). Unrelentingly atonal from the start (ten out of the 12 chromatic notes are used in the first phrase alone), the piece rises to an anguished climax, marked *ffff*, before its muted ending. What private thoughts the prodigious 16-year-old had while playing to himself this unhomely music we can only guess.

Go Play, Boy, Play

It should not come as a surprise that Britten found the Royal College a disappointing place. *The attitude of most of the RCM students was amateurish and folksy*, he wrote in 1959. *That made me feel highly intolerant.*[28] His later memories were no doubt coloured by an overall feeling that the College had not done justice to his talent. Certainly he had reason to complain that only two pieces of his – a Phantasy string quintet and the *Sinfonietta* – were played publicly there during his three years as a student. And the College offered no sense of liberation from his schoolboy life, as a university might have done; it seemed more like a continuation of it, and consequently Britten's growing-up was delayed for another three years – and more.

The Royal College of Music in Kensington had in fact been founded in 1883 to provide a more thoroughly professional training than the older Royal Academy. The Academy had produced few noteworthy composers in recent years, whereas Vaughan Williams, Holst, Ireland, Bridge and Tippett had all attended the College in the first 40 years of its existence. So despite Britten's criticism, it was still almost certainly the best institution on offer. Bridge had probably made the wisest comment in a thoughtful letter he wrote to Britten shortly before he went to the RCM – a letter in which he recommended John Ireland as a composition teacher: 'Personally I think an institution only helps one to find one's feet'.[29]

Harold Samuel had recommended R O Morris, a notable teacher of counterpoint who was at this time giving private post-graduate lessons in fugal technique to Tippett; but Bridge, who had been Ireland's contemporary at the College, suggested that it

In cricket whites, South Lodge, 1933

would be preferable to 'plump for a live composer whose activities are part of the present-day outlook with a heavy leaning towards tomorrow's!' He added: 'I think you may have to do a certain amount of work to sharpen up your technique, which may appear to you, at first, as being a retrograde step.'[30] Ireland duly became Britten's composition teacher and, as Bridge had prophesied, he immediately set Britten to work on exercises in strict counterpoint and fugue, and then got him to write a mass in the style of Palestrina. But he was not a very reliable teacher: he failed to turn up for their first lesson, and when Britten later visited his house the puritanical boy was shocked by the squalor of Ireland's Bohemian life. He told his sister Beth that he would sometimes find Ireland still in bed, with a hangover, and on one occasion he was *quite drunk . . . foully so.*[31] Britten admired some of Ireland's works at first, though he soon became critical, and ended up (as did Frank Bridge) more or less writing him off.

His piano teacher at the College was Arthur Benjamin (1893–1960), a composer too, known today principally for his *Jamaican Rumba*, but whose comic opera *The Devil Take Her* earned warm praise from Britten. Benjamin was a friendly Australian and the two got on well immediately, even if Benjamin was critical of

Britten's playing technique and soon told him that he was not cut out to be a solo pianist: *how I'm going to make my pennies Heaven only knows*,[33] was Britten's diary comment. Benjamin was right in that Britten never did become a professional soloist, although in 1938 he did give the first performance of his Piano Concerto. He became, of course, an accompanist of the highest quality, one of the finest there has ever been. Britten always remained on good terms with Benjamin: he dedicated his light-hearted piano suite *Holiday Diary* to his teacher and in the 1934 letter

John Ireland (1879–1962) studied piano with Frederic Cliffe and composition with Charles Stanford at the Royal College of Music, where he taught composition from 1920 to 1939. Besides Britten his pupils included Alan Bush and E J Moeran. Ireland's music has a distinctive English feeling, nourished by his attraction to particular places and landscapes, especially in Sussex where he lived at the end of his life. His orchestral music includes the tone poems *The Forgotten Rite* (1913) and *Mai-Dun* (1910–11) and the Piano Concerto (1930), written for Helen Perkin, whom Britten referred to in his diary as *Ireland's star & best comp. pupil*,[32] and with whom Ireland was in love at the time.

in which he suggests the dedication he offers *Infinite thanks for what you are doing & have done for me.*[34]

Apart from weekly lessons with his teachers, Britten was largely free to compose and practise, and in the evenings to go to concerts, some of them at the adjacent Royal Albert Hall. For his first year he lived in a boarding house in Bayswater, across the park from the College, *rather a nice place but rather full of old ladies*;[35] then in September 1931 he moved to new lodgings a few minutes' walk from the RCM, sharing them with his sister Beth, who was learning dressmaking. His other sister Barbara was also in London, working as a health visitor, and Britten saw a lot of her too. Ben and Barbara were both members of the English Madrigal Choir, in spite of his bass voice being somewhat uncertain – the only one of his musical attributes that was not outstanding. Singing madrigals seems to have had an immediate influence on his music: the first major chamber piece he wrote at the College was a string quartet in D major whose lyrical melodic lines are in striking contrast to his recent experiments in Expressionism, and which he was to have published in revised form shortly before his death.

In his diary comments on concerts he often expresses irritation with his English contemporaries and predecessors. He had always found Elgar dull, and nothing he heard in these days made him change his mind. He did finally come to terms with Elgar towards the end of his life, conducting the *Introduction and Allegro* at the 1969 Aldeburgh Festival and recording *The Dream of Gerontius* with Peter Pears in 1971. Hearing Vaughan Williams's *Tallis Fantasia*, he found it *v. beautiful (wonderfully scored)*,[36] but had little good to say about anything else of his. Bax's *November Woods* bored him (*not much November about it*).[37] His huge admiration for Brahms, whom through his teenage years he had ranked second only to Beethoven, gradually waned, perhaps under the influence of fellow RCM students. By July 1934 he could write in his diary of Vaughan Williams's *Benedicite – music which repulses me as does most of Brahms (solid, dull)*.[38] But he was also hearing all kinds of stimulating new music: Stravinsky's *Sacre du printemps* on first hearing was *bewildering & terrifying. I didn't really enjoy it, but I think it's incredibly marvellous & arresting*,[39] and his *Symphony of Psalms* was *Marvellous . . . the end was truly inspired*.[40] A performance of Schoenberg's *Erwartung* under the composer's baton was baffling (*I could not make head or tail of it*),[41] but Walton's Viola Concerto was *a great turning point in my musical life*,[42] as he wrote in a 1963 letter to Walton.

His foremost discovery at this time, however, was Mahler, who was to become one of his most kindred spirits. Another was Schubert: in both composers he would have sensed the child's vision to which the music always reaches back. An affinity with Mahler is already apparent in the nine-year-old Britten's 'Beware': although he could not possibly have heard any of his music at that time, it sounds astonishingly like an early Mahler song, even ending with the classic Mahlerian device of the major triad fading to a minor one. His first actual encounter with Mahler's music was a performance of the Fourth Symphony (the shortest) at a BBC Promenade Concert in September 1930, just before he started at the College, and on which he commented laconically in his diary: *Much too long, but beautiful in pts.*[43] Twelve years later, he wrote about that first experience, perhaps with the hindsight of now knowing the work very well: *the scoring startled me. It was mainly 'soloistic' and entirely clean and transparent. The colouring seemed calculated to the smallest shade, and the result was wonderfully resonant . . . the material was remarkable, and the melodic shapes highly original, with such rhythmic and harmonic tension from beginning to end. After that concert, I made every effort to hear Mahler's music.*[44] A few months later he bought a score of the *Lieder eines fahrenden Gesellen*, and heard the work at a BBC Symphony Orchestra concert in May 1931 (*Lovely little pieces, exquisitely scored – a lesson to all the Elgars & Strausses in the world*).[45] He probably studied other Mahler orchestral scores at the RCM that summer: his ballet score *Plymouth Town*, composed in the autumn of 1931 but never performed in his lifetime, shows the influence of Mahler in its orchestration; at one point Britten asks the oboes and clarinets to play 'bells up' – an indication he could only have seen in Mahler's symphonies.

He soon changed his mind about the Fourth Symphony's length, and this became a favourite Mahler work of his, which he eventually conducted at the 1961 Aldeburgh Festival (a performance that survives in a BBC recording). But the piece that was to make the greatest impression on him was *Das Lied von der Erde*. He first heard this on the radio in February 1936, and the

Letter to Henry Boys (1910–92), 29 June 1937:

It is now well past midnight & society dictates that I should stop playing the Abschied. Otherwise I might possibly have gone on repeating the last record indefinitely – for 'ewig' keit of course.

It is cruel, you know, that music should be so beautiful. It has the beauty of loneliness & of pain: of strength & freedom. The beauty of disappointment & never-satisfied love. The cruel beauty of nature, and everlasting beauty of monotony.

And the essentially 'pretty' colours of the normal orchestral palette are used to paint this extraordinary picture of loneliness. And there is nothing morbid about it. The same harmonic progressions that Wagner used to colour his essentially morbid love-scenes (his 'Liebes' is naturally followed by 'Tod') are used here to paint a serenity literally supernatural. I cannot understand it – it passes over me like a tidal wave – and that matters not a jot either, because it goes on for ever, even if it is never performed again – that final chord is printed on the atmosphere.

Perhaps if I could understand some of the Indian philosophies I might approach it a little. At the moment I can do no more than bask in its Heavenly light – & it is worth having lived to do that.

inadequacy of the performance and his irritation at its being sung in English still *couldn't dim the beauties of this heavenly work. Was there ever such a touching Lebewohl as this? This music makes one think furiously more than any other today.*[46] The impact of the 'Abschied' from *Das Lied* in particular may be heard in *Our Hunting Fathers*, which he was writing at the time. The lean, chamber scoring in *Das Lied* was a continuing influence, right up to *Death in Venice*. *Das Lied* too, with its settings of Chinese poetry, its use of pentatonic scales and, in the 'Abschied', of heterophony, was Britten's first contact with the oriental world and a profound musical response to it, which was to have huge repercussions in his later life. In 1937 he bought the famous Bruno Walter live recording with the Vienna Philharmonic, and wrote an extraordinarily insightful letter about it to his friend Henry Boys.

It should be emphasized that Britten was in the vanguard of Mahler lovers in the England of the 1930s: most of the critics then, and the public, had no time for this 'tolerable imitation of a composer',[47] as Vaughan Williams called him – a situation that continued right up to the centenary of Mahler's birth in 1960, after which there was a dramatic change. Britten must have been sad that he could never convince Frank Bridge about the worth of Mahler's music: *We are in complete agreement over all – except Mahler! – though he admits he is a great thinker*,[48] he wrote in his diary in March 1936. During his RCM years he saw a great deal of Bridge, whom he still considered his real teacher; they often went to concerts together and compared notes on new pieces they heard. In June 1931, the 17-year-old Britten made his first visit to the Bridges' weekend cottage at Friston, near Eastbourne in Sussex: he played tennis, enjoyed the surrounding downland countryside, and met their next-door neighbour, the artist Marjorie Fass, who became a friend and confidante. He made a few friends among his fellow students, notably Remo Lauricella, a violinist, and Bernard Richards, a cellist: he played piano trios with the two of them. One friendship, with a fellow bass in the English Madrigal Choir, Paul Wright, led to his meeting with Iris Lemare, a conductor, and Anne Macnaghten, the leader of an all-female string quartet, who together with the composer Elisabeth Lutyens founded the Macnaghten-Lemare Concerts. From the beginning of 1932 these concerts presented new British works at a tiny theatre in Notting Hill Gate. Since the RCM students seemed largely unable to cope with Britten's music, the Macnaghten-Lemare Concerts were a compensating opportunity for him. In the second series they played his Phantasy Quintet for strings, which had won the Cobbett Prize – an annual award for chamber pieces endowed by Walter Cobbett, a rich businessman and amateur musician – and also received a College performance (*bad – but I expected worse*);[49] three Walter de la Mare part-songs, the first work of his to get into print; and most importantly, the first public performance of his *Sinfonietta*, which Britten designated, finally, as his Opus 1, and dedicated to Bridge.

The *Sinfonietta*, composed in a little under three weeks during June and July 1932, is the culmination of all the chamber pieces he had been writing throughout his teens. Its scoring – for wind quintet plus string quintet – is quite similar to that of Schoenberg's First Chamber Symphony, to which Britten pays homage with the rising horn motif near the start. Schoenberg also served as the model for Britten's thematic economy and the way he develops and transforms his material throughout the piece, yet stylistically Schoenberg's influence is hardly discernible. The second movement, like much of the music that Britten was writing while he was at the College, has an English pastoral feeling about it, though it is more tightly composed than Ireland or Vaughan Williams. The tarantella finale is the most Brittenish movement, the first outstanding example of those hectic dances in his early music that seem to display nervous rather than physical energy. The *Sinfonietta* has a cool, steely brilliance that perhaps excites more admiration than affection. Those early critics who (to his intense annoyance) characterized Britten's music as 'clever but superficial' were mistaken, although they had a point. It is perhaps because Britten at this time had a restricted emotional life that much of his early music lacks real warmth: he was still the brilliant boy who had yet to grow up.

His Opus 2, the Phantasy for oboe and string trio, is a more immediately attractive and incisive work than the *Sinfonietta*, perhaps because its manner, though equally skilful, is less self-conscious. The Englishness of the *Sinfonietta*'s slow movement is also apparent in the Phantasy's central section, music for string trio of considerable tenderness and finesse. This manner was not to be pursued any further, unlike the shadowy march music that begins the Phantasy. Britten became rather obsessed with the march form over the next few years.

His next project was a large-scale suite for string quartet called *Alla Quartetto Serioso*, to which he gave the whimsical subtitle '*Go play, boy, play'* – a quotation from *The Winter's Tale*. There was no programmatic connection with Shakespeare: Britten probably just liked the words for their association with school – the piece was to have been a series of portraits of school friends and evocations of school activities. He finished four of the projected five movements (one of them only sketched), and these gave him considerable trouble as he worked on them intermittently over three years, from 1933 to 1936. He replaced the original 'Alla marcia' (which was later reborn as 'Parade' in *Les Illuminations*) with a more forceful march full of Bartókian glissandi. The three completed movements were performed at a Macnaghten-Lemare concert in December 1933, rather against Britten's wishes; he was unhappy enough to leave the concert without thanking Anne Macnaghten and the quartet. In their final state they were played by the Stratton Quartet at the Wigmore Hall in 1936 as *Three Divertimenti*, where they were received *with sniggers and pretty cold silence.*[50] This was enough to make Britten lose faith in the work altogether, as on several other later occasions. Throughout his life Britten was to combine extremes of self-confidence and self-doubt, and the latter could so easily prevail over the former. His fine *Temporal Variations* for oboe and piano, however, which received a single performance later in 1936, was put back on the shelf not because of bad reviews but, apparently, because of a disagreement with one of the players.

Even though he abandoned *'Go play, boy, play'*, it was an important stepping stone. Its school associations may be backward-looking, yet much of its music points forward. The March is inherently dramatic, and its fanfares anticipate *Les Illuminations*; the waltz in the second movement is not simply a waltz but a study of the form: a 'waltz'. The idea of the 'character piece' was again something that became important to him in his post-RCM years.

His attitude to modernism fluctuated. In February 1933, at the

Queen's Hall with Frank Bridge, he heard Schoenberg's *Variations for Orchestra* conducted by the composer, and found the piece *rather dull* (an astonishing remark!), *but some good things in it.*[51] He adds, tantalizingly, *Meet Sch. in interval* – without further comment. At the end of 1933, when he had passed the Associateship of the RCM with his accustomed ease and had been awarded a £100 travelling scholarship, he hoped to go to Vienna to study with Alban Berg. Frank Bridge would certainly have encouraged him to do so: Britten had been impressed both by the *Lyric Suite* (*astounding . . . The imagination & intense emotion of this work certainly amaze me*)[52] and the *Three Fragments from Wozzeck* which he had heard earlier in the year, and would probably have known other Berg pieces from scores. In 1963 he described what happened next: *. . . when the College was told, coolness arose. I think, but can't be sure, that the director, Sir Hugh Allen, put a spike in the wheel. At any rate, when I said at home during the holidays, 'I am going to study with Berg, aren't I?' the answer was a firm 'No, dear.' Pressed, my mother said, 'He's not a good influence', which I suspect came from Allen. There was at that time an almost moral prejudice against serial music – which makes one smile today! I think also that there was some confusion in my parents' minds – thinking that 'not a good influence' meant morally, not musically. They had been disturbed by traits of rebelliousness and unconventionality which I had shown in my later school days.*[53] What kind of composer Britten would have become if he had studied with Berg is impossible to say. Certainly he remained attached to Berg's music all his life. He was deeply affected by Berg's premature death in 1935: *I feel it is a real & terrible tragedy – one from which the world will take long to recover from,*[54] he wrote to Marjorie Fass. He attended the premiere of Berg's Violin Concerto at the ISCM Festival in Barcelona in 1936 and found it *just shattering*;[55] on buying the score later that year he wrote in his diary *My God what a sublime work!*[56]

The truth is that even though Britten was more thoroughly

aware than almost any of his contemporaries of the Schoenbergian revolution and had himself become quite adept in a virtually atonal style, he was destined to be a tonal composer who, more than any other, would prove the truth of Schoenberg's assertion that there was plenty of good music still to be written in C major – and did so at a time when many composers' belief in tonality was faltering. The best and most personal music he was composing as a student is the most openly diatonic. In his later music he would occasionally flirt with Schoenbergian serialism by using a 12-note row as a constructive device – in *The Turn of the Screw*, *A Midsummer Night's Dream*, *Cantata Academica*, *Owen Wingrave* and *Death in Venice* – but whereas the intention of Schoenberg's 12-note method was to move completely beyond tonality, Britten's rows always have strong tonal implications. The main work he was writing during 1933, *A Boy was Born*, inhabits a world as far from Berg and from Schoenbergian Expressionism as it is possible to imagine. In various pieces written over the previous ten years, Britten had been working out a fresh relation to the English choral tradition. Lately, as a singer in the English Madrigal Choir and the Carlyle Singers to which he also belonged, the relation had become an active one. *A Boy was Born* sets a sequence of (mostly medieval) poems on the theme of Christmas, in the form of a theme and six variations. With the sound of the all-male English cathedral choir in mind, Britten employs treble voices for the first time, thus inaugurating a whole series of works in which boys take part. The use of voices is one of the most distinctive features of his sound world. At this time Britten was still a practising Christian, so the words he set had real meaning for him. The music is certainly inspired, and sounds consistently new and fresh, nowhere more so than in the fifth variation, a combination of Christina Rossetti's 'In the Bleak Midwinter' and the 16th-century Corpus Christi Carol. The passage where the boys enter with 'He bare him up, he bare him down / He bare him into an orchard brown' in a flowing 12/8 over the women's gently dissonant overlapping phrases on the words 'snow on snow' is the moment when, at the age of 19, Britten reveals himself as a true genius instead of (merely!) a remarkable talent.

He dedicated the work to his father, who was ill with lymphatic cancer, though this was not yet diagnosed. The BBC, who were already aware of Britten's potential, recorded the piece for broadcasting. Victor Hely-Hutchinson, one of many composers on the Corporation's music staff (Britten had described his *Carol Symphony* as *utter bilge*[57] after hearing it on the radio in December 1932), had written in a memorandum in June 1933: 'I do wholeheartedly subscribe to the general opinion that Mr Britten is the most interesting new arrival since Walton, and I feel we should watch his work very carefully.'[58] The broadcast of *A Boy was Born* took place on 23 February 1934. By a remarkable and significant coincidence, this was the day of Elgar's death.

Coldest Love Will Warm to Action

At the beginning of 1934 Britten was 20 and his formal education was over. He was back in the family house in Lowestoft, determined to begin his career as a professional musician. He had one publisher and was soon to switch to another: Ralph Hawkes of Boosey & Hawkes agreed to take over the *Sinfonietta* and the Phantasy Quartet from OUP. They were to publish all his subsequent music until the 1960s. Faced with the responsibility of earning his living, however, he found himself in a creative block. On 3 January he wrote to his composer friend Grace Williams, whom he had met through the Macnaghten-Lemare concerts: *I cannot write a single note of anything respectable at the moment, and so – on the off chance of making some money – I am dishing up some very old stuff (written, some of it, over ten years ago) as a dear little school suite for strings.*[59] This was the *Simple Symphony*, which he conducted with an amateur orchestra in Norwich in March. At the end of the month he set off with a school friend from South Lodge, John Pounder, for the International Society of Contemporary Music Festival at Florence, where his Phantasy was being played by its dedicatee, Leon Goossens, and members of the Griller Quartet. In Florence he met the conductor Hermann Scherchen, who was to have conducted the *Sinfonietta* in Strasbourg the previous year (the performance was cancelled) and his 14-year-old son Wulff; they were staying in the same *pensione* as Britten and Pounder. Britten made a day trip to Siena with the Scherchens; during a rainstorm he and Wulff shared a mackintosh, and a rapport immediately sprang up between them that was to assume much greater significance a few years later.

The following day he received a telegram from his mother

summoning him home: 'Pop not so well'. In fact Robert Britten had already died of a cerebral haemorrhage: he was 57. His father's death brought Britten even closer to his mother. In the weeks following the funeral he stayed with her at the school where his brother Robert was now headmaster, in Prestatyn, North Wales. He began writing a set of songs with piano for the boys to sing, which was published as *Friday Afternoons* – Friday being the day on which Robert took singing practice. The world of children and school was still his only real subject; he was cocooned in his sequestered adolescence. But the vein of simple lyricism he was cultivating – as in the delightful 'Sailing' from the *Holidays* Suite – was perhaps the truest of his voices. In looking back over his boyhood pieces in order to put together the *Simple Symphony*, did he realize that his ability to invent unselfconscious melody – which he still possessed – was his most precious gift?

In October he and his mother went to Vienna, via Basel and Salzburg. Britten had hoped to meet Berg in Vienna, but he was away. He did, however, meet Erwin Stein, an editor at Universal Edition, who ten years later was to become his personal editor at Boosey & Hawkes and a loyal supporter of his music. Stein had been a pupil of Schoenberg and was a Mahler disciple; he and Britten would have had much to discuss. Britten was enchanted with Vienna, and especially with its opera. He immersed himself in Wagner: *The five hours of* [*Die Meistersinger*] *didn't seem as many minutes; the incredible vitality, richness: lovely melody, humour, pathos in fact every favourable quality,*[60] he wrote in his diary. While in Vienna he began his Suite, Op 6, for violin and piano, one of the most brilliant and accomplished of his early works. There are several Viennese features: the totally chromatic style of the Introduction continues his fascination with Schoenberg, while the finale is an elaborate and showy Waltz. In between come a March – a scintillating example of this favourite form – and a beautiful Lullaby, Britten's first great evocation of sleep's healing power.

'The Three Graces': Auden, Coldstream, Britten, the Downs School, Colwall, June 1936

Returning to England, he was soon living once again in London. Here he found a temporary solution to his career problem. As a result of a recommendation by the BBC, he was approached at the end of April 1935 by the General Post Office's Film Unit to write music for a documentary film called *The King's Stamp*, about the making of a special stamp for King George V's Silver Jubilee. The film was directed by the painter William Coldstream. Despite misgivings about what he called *this God-forsaken subject*, Britten accepted the job. He was now something of a cinema aficionado, and so had an immediate understanding of what was needed. Over the next year and a half he would write music for 25 films, the majority short documentaries, but also one feature film, *Love from a Stranger*. The GPO Film Unit, for whom most of his scores were written, was a group of young artists and intellectuals, headed by the noted documentary film-maker John Grierson. Almost all of them held the strong left-wing opinions prevailing at the time. The unit encouraged innovation, and Britten was only too willing to experiment with sound effects in devising his incidental music. His next assignment after *The King's Stamp* was *Coal Face*, a film about miners at work. W H Auden was approached to write some words for Britten to set, and the two of them met at the Downs

School at Colwall in Herefordshire, where Auden taught. *Auden is the most amazing man, a very brilliant and attractive personality*,[61] Britten recorded in his diary. Britten seemed very young to Auden, who was six years older than him, but Auden soon recognized his exceptional musicality and included him in the 'gang' of artists, who under Auden's leadership were to take on the world. He, Spender and Cecil Day Lewis were the gang's designated poets, Christopher Isherwood was the novelist, Coldstream was the painter, and Britten now became the composer. Auden took Britten to the Westminster Theatre to see the Group Theatre's productions of his plays *The Dance of Death* and *The Dog Beneath the Skin* (the latter co-written with Isherwood), and introduced Britten to members of the gang, including Isherwood and his Group Theatre friends, the director Rupert Doone and his partner, the designer Robert Medley. In fact virtually all the gang were homosexual or bisexual. It was essentially through his

W H Auden (1907–73) was the outstanding English poet of his generation. His first volume of poems was published in 1930, and from then on he had a huge influence on his contemporaries, who included Stephen Spender, Cecil Day Lewis and Louis MacNeice. His poetry of the 1930s, drawing on insights from, amongst others, Freud and D H Lawrence, dealt with all aspects of contemporary life, using intensely individual imagery to express universal truths. He moved to New York in 1939 and took US citizenship in 1946. Auden's later poetry does not have the same immediacy and force as his earlier work (the Christianity that he espoused from the 1940s tended to soften its edge), but is always wide-ranging in scope and innovative in its language. With Chester Kallman, Auden wrote opera librettos for Stravinsky (*The Rake's Progress*, 1951) and Henze (*Elegy for Young Lovers*, 1959; *The Bassarids*, 1963). In 1972 he returned to England, where he was given a cottage in the grounds of Christ Church, Oxford, his old college. Since 1957 he had spent his summers in Austria, and he died in Vienna in September 1973.

friendship with Auden, which soon became a close one, that Britten finally came to acknowledge the fact that he was homosexual himself.

For the time being, his friendships with boys and young men were still quite innocent. He formed a strong attachment to a teenager, Piers Dunkerley, who had been at South Lodge School, and took him to films and plays. But Britten's puritanism and the continuing inhibiting presence of his mother presumably combined to prevent any amorous intentions he might have had from going further. (Dunkerley was later to become a Captain in the Royal Marines during the Second World War. In 1959 he committed suicide. He was one of the four dedicatees of the *War Requiem*.) Meanwhile Auden, whose attitude to sex was cheerfully and guiltlessly promiscuous, encouraged Britten to be more open about his inclinations, at first without success. A poem Auden sent to Britten, 'Night covers up the rigid land' might appear to suggest that he was in love with him – though at the time Auden was deeply in love with someone else. Another poem Auden wrote for Britten, 'Underneath the abject willow', spells out his advice with eloquent directness. Britten set both these poems to music, 'Underneath the abject willow' for two voices and piano in a detached and almost flippant manner that seems like a mild reproof to Auden's earnestness.

Assuming the didactic role he was accustomed to take with his friends, Auden also acted as Britten's intellectual and political mentor. Britten's politics changed from a fairly unthinking conservatism to an emotional commitment to socialism and especially pacifism, which he was to retain for the rest of his life. His diary entries at this time become filled with despairing comments on Italy's aggression in Abyssinia, and the Spanish Civil War. He found Auden and his friends intimidating at times, as his March 1937 diary also reveals. *They* [Auden, Isherwood and Coldstream] *are nice people – but I am not up to their mark tonight, feeling dazed, stupid & incredibly miserable – & so leave them at 9.0 with an over-whelming inferiority complex & longing for bed.*[62] It was hard for him to acknowledge that in his own way he was quite Auden's equal, and that both of them in fact had a similar cast of mind – which is why their collaboration over the next few years was so fruitful; but it was also perhaps why, at the point when Britten realized that he needed to be more independent, the relationship faltered.

Britten's first important collaboration with Auden was the GPO film *Night Mail*, for which Auden provided the famous lines beginning 'This is the night mail crossing the border, Bringing the cheque and the postal order'. Britten took his task of imitating train noises very seriously (as a boy, he had been a keen train-spotter). He spent an evening beside the railway line at Harrow, and tried to reproduce on an assortment of improvised percussion instruments the sounds he had heard. The percussionist at the recording session was James Blades, who was to go on working with Britten on a

Underneath the abject willow,
  Lover, sulk no more;
Act from thought should quickly follow:
  What is thinking for?
Your unique and moping station
  Proves you cold;
  Stand up and fold
Your map of desolation.

Bells that toll across the meadows
  From the sombre spire,
Toll for those unloving shadows
  Love does not require.
All that lives may love; why longer
  Bow to loss
  With arms across?
Strike and you shall conquer.

Geese in flocks above you flying
  Their direction know;
Brooks beneath the thin ice flowing
  To their oceans go;
Coldest love will warm to action,
  Walk then, come,
  No longer numb,
Into your satisfaction.
(W H Auden)

variety of innovative percussion effects until the end of the composer's life. The film, like *Coal Face* a milestone in the history of documentaries, was a success with the audience when first shown in March 1936.

By this time Auden and Britten were working on a more ambitious project: an orchestral song-cycle for the Norwich Triennial Festival that autumn. This was *Our Hunting Fathers*, in which poems about animals were used metaphorically to lament in general the misguided notions of human superiority that had led mankind to its present sorry state; and to make a particular comment on the current political situation, where the strong were brutally persecuting the weak. Britten does this most pointedly in Thomas Ravenscroft's 'Hawking the Partridge', retitled 'Dance of Death', a hunting piece in which he juxtaposes two of the hawks' names, 'German' and 'Jew' in a way that no perceptive listener could fail to understand. Two recent discoveries particularly affected the music: Mahler's *Das Lied von der Erde*, and a contemporary of Britten's who had also been influenced by Mahler – Shostakovich. Britten had attended a concert performance of *Lady Macbeth of the Mtsensk District* in March and wrote an admiring account of it in his diary: *I will defend it through thick & thin against these charges of 'lack of style' . . . The 'eminent English Renaissance' composers sniggering in the stalls was typical. There is more music in a page of MacBeth than in the whole of their 'elegant' output!*[63] The immediate impact of *Lady Macbeth* can be heard in the brass band piece *Russian Funeral* which Britten wrote for the Communist composer Alan Bush and the London Labour Choral Union, and whose main theme is coincidentally a Russian folksong that Shostakovich was later to use in his 11th Symphony. Mahler's influence on *Our Hunting Fathers* is most obviously heard in 'Messalina', with its lamenting high woodwind lines, and also in the closing 'Epilogue and Funeral March'; but the xylophone ostinato that creeps through the texture of the latter is clearly indebted to Shostakovich, as is some of the satirical tone of the music.

The premiere of *Our Hunting Fathers* in September 1936 was an ordeal for Britten. He conducted, and at the first rehearsal with the London Philharmonic Orchestra, some of the musicians misbehaved disgracefully. Sophie Wyss, the soprano soloist, recalled how during 'Rats Away!' – a medieval imprecation on a plague of rats, set by Britten as a wild *Allegro con fuoco* – the players 'ran about pretending they were chasing rats on the floor!'[64] Things improved in Norwich the next day, and the performance went fairly well. The audience was polite but clearly discomfited. They had already found the new piece in the first half of the concert unsettling, Vaughan Williams's *Five Tudor Portraits* with its uncharacteristically bawdy Skelton text. After this, Auden's provocative words and the apparently bizarre new sounds of Britten's music must have thoroughly upset them. Even Frank Bridge was doubtful, and Mrs Britten, who had heard relatively little of her son's recent music, commented to a friend: 'Oh, I do hope Ben will write something that somebody will like.'[65] Britten had already played through 'Rats Away!' to her on the piano and was secretly pleased that she thoroughly disapproved of it, as he was now half-consciously trying to break away from her influence. She had turned to Christian Science, the sect founded by Mary Baker Eddy which believed that illness could be cured by prayer. Britten found this inimical, and he himself had given up church attendance since his conversion to left-wing politics.

Britten had reason to be proud of *Our Hunting Fathers*: it is a score of extraordinary virtuosity, and it is hard to believe this was the first orchestral music of his own he had ever heard played. Despite its mixed reception, the performance must surely have boosted his confidence. He was, however, to retreat from the provocative stance he and Auden had taken. Mrs Britten had hit on a partial truth: he did want to be liked. *Épater le bourgeois* was a temporary need, but he would soon be glad to win the middle classes over to his side.

In October he moved with Beth to a new London flat in the Finchley Road, and returned to writing film and theatre music. He wrote, in a few days, a score to the feature film *Love from a Stranger*, starring Basil Rathbone; its title music was influenced by Mahler's Fifth Symphony (as was the later storm music from *Peter Grimes*). There was a room in the flat for his mother to stay in when she visited, and in the new year, when both he and Beth became ill with 'flu, his mother came to nurse them, only to fall ill herself. Barbara now took charge, and a professional nurse was engaged when first Beth and then Mrs Britten developed pneumonia. While Benjamin recovered and Beth was now out of danger, Edith's condition deteriorated rapidly. On 31 January 1937 she had a heart attack and died. *Nothing one can do eases the terrible ache that one feels,*[66] he wrote in his diary, with a curious use of the impersonal pronoun. But he was certainly devastated, and it was a long time before he fully recovered from the shock, especially as he also blamed himself for some time afterwards for being the indirect cause of her fatal illness. Yet his mother's death was also a great liberation for him.

On 5 March 1937, just over a month after her death, his diary records: *I lunch with David Green* [an architect friend, also from Lowestoft] *who is very decent – & he emphasizes the point (very truly) that now is the time for me to decide something about my sexual life. O, for a little courage!* We cannot tell for how long he had known he was homosexual, but it would appear that his response to his mother's obsessive love had effectively barred him from sexual feelings towards other women. In 1915 Freud noted a common pattern in the homosexuals he had observed: 'in the earliest years of their childhood, [they] pass through a phase of very intense but short-lived fixation to a woman (usually their mother), and . . . after leaving this behind, they identify themselves with a woman and take *themselves* as their sexual object. That is to say, proceeding from a basis of narcissism, they look for a young man who resembles themselves and whom *they* may love as their mother loved *them*.'[67] Whether or not Freud's observation is universally true, Britten's sexual development seems to have proceeded closely along these lines. As a teenager he had been attracted to younger boys from South Lodge School, but had sublimated any sexual feelings into those of fraternal and later quasi-paternal care. Donald Mitchell cogently sums up his emotional life before his mother died: 'all the evidence points to her son existing in a strange kind of void, in which the most intense human relationships were extensions – or perhaps attempted replicas – of the friendships and above all the hierarchies of school.'[68] There are occasional hints of self-awareness: *tell it not in Gath*,[69] Britten writes at the beginning of his 1936 diary of his friendship with Piers Dunkerley, referring to the biblical David and Jonathan; and a month later, after a train journey to London: *Have some tea on the journey & some buns, but rather because of the nice little restaurant-boy who brings it & talks a bit. Quel horreur!! But I swear there's no harm in it.*[70]

Quel horreur is characteristic: Britten's puritanism was still a powerful inhibition. Visiting Barcelona in the spring of 1936, where he and Antonio Brosa played his Suite for violin and piano at the ISCM Festival, he visited the red-light district with Lennox Berkeley, another featured composer he had met at the Festival, and a young critic, Peter Burra. Britten was shocked by the *sordidity – & the sexual temptations of every kind at each corner*.[71] One cannot help thinking here of Picasso's rather different attitude to Barcelona's brothels! Britten writes similarly about a visit, shortly before his mother died, to a brothel in Paris with Henry Boys and Ronald Duncan, a young writer he had recently met and befriended: *we . . . are presented in the most sordid manner possible with about 20 nude females, fat, hairy, unprepossessing . . . It is revolting – appalling that such a noble thing as sex should be so degraded.*[72] The constant emphasis in his music on innocence, and the horror of innocence being corrupted, points both to his idealistic puritanism but perhaps also to a darker side within his own experience, of which we cannot be certain, but to which he himself referred in conversation with two of his librettists who were also close friends. Britten revealed to Eric Crozier that he had been sexually abused at South Lodge School by the headmaster, Thomas Sewell; he also told Myfanwy Piper that his father had homosexual inclinations, and had sent him out to procure boys. The first story may be an exaggeration or a distortion of his or his friends' experience of being beaten: we do know that Sewell had something of

Ronald Duncan (1914–82) was a prolific writer of poetry, plays and other literary works. He first met Britten in 1935 and collaborated with him on a *Pacifist March* for the Peace Pledge Union. By the 1940s he was a successful playwright. Britten wrote incidental music for his plays *This Way to the Tomb* and *Stratton*. Duncan also wrote a cantata text, *Amo Ergo Sum*, which Britten set to music for the wedding of Lord Harewood to Erwin Stein's daughter Marion in 1949. But Duncan is best remembered as the librettist of *The Rape of Lucretia*. He wrote a memoir, *Working with Britten*, which, if somewhat free with the facts, is full of insights and touching memories of their close, though difficult friendship.

a fixation – not uncommon at that time – on beating boys. It is also possible that Britten's horror of sadism and of violence in general concealed a repressed attraction to both. The second story sounds, on the face of it, preposterous, and may have been pure fantasy – but it is worth recording if only because Britten *did* relate it.[73] Certainly there are other hints that the Britten family life was not the untroubled and happy one that it was supposed to be, and Mr Britten's real character is puzzling. So much around Britten's upbringing remains – and will probably always remain – secret and unknown.

If this story *was* fantasy, a psychoanalytic explanation might be that Britten was attempting to transfer some of his own guilt about his attraction to boys on to his father. That he did feel guilt is certain: his last opera *Death in Venice* spells out very clearly his mature attitude towards this side of his sexuality. In the present climate of intense suspicion about paedophilia there is a tendency to suppose that anyone who falls in love with boys will abuse them; but Britten's strong moral sense always acted as a constraint, however insistent his feelings may sometimes have been. Moreover, a large part of his lifelong attraction to children and teenagers can be related to his unfulfilled desire for children of his own. *I am getting to such a condition that I am lost without children (of either sex) near me*,[74] he records revealingly in another diary entry from 1936 about Piers Dunkerley.

In July 1936 while Britten was on holiday in Cornwall finishing *Our Hunting Fathers*, Lennox Berkeley visited him there. He was ten years older than Britten and a fine pianist. He and Britten found their musical tastes were very similar. Berkeley was at this time having a homosexual affair with José Raffalli (he eventually

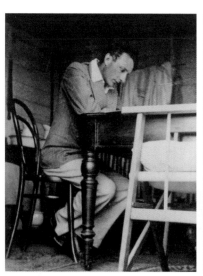

Berkeley and Britten working, Crantock, Cornwall, summer 1936

married and his son, Michael, became Britten's godson and a composer) and he may have wanted to begin an affair then with Britten. If so, Britten discouraged him, continuing to stay aloof the next spring when he stayed with Berkeley in Gloucestershire, during which visit they composed a joint orchestral work, *Mont Juic*, based on Catalan folk songs. *He is a dear & I am very, very fond of him, nevertheless, it is a comfort that we can arrange sexual matters at least to my satisfaction*,[75] he confided to his diary. Britten was also seeing Peter Burra, and was attracted to him, though again he held back. Then on 27 April 1937 Burra was killed when a small plane in which he was flying with a friend crashed. In helping to sort out Burra's possessions, Britten got to know another of his friends, a young singer he had met briefly at a lunch party a few weeks before: Peter Pears.

Lennox Berkeley (1903–89) was born into an aristocratic family of partly French ancestry. He attended Gresham's School a decade before Britten was there and went on to read French at Oxford. On Ravel's advice, he went to Paris to study composition with Nadia Boulanger, and his music, tasteful and sophisticated, always retained French rather than English manners. He became a Roman Catholic in 1928 and wrote a large quantity of religious music. His large-scale works include four operas, two of which, *A Dinner Engagement* (1954) and *Castaway* (1967) were premiered at the Aldeburgh Festival. He was professor of composition at the Royal Academy of Music from 1946 to 1968, where his pupils included Richard Rodney Bennett, Nicholas Maw and John Tavener.

Peter Pears was born in 1910. His family were rather grander than Britten's, and unlike Britten he spent most of his childhood away from his parents, who were frequently abroad. Nevertheless, he was deeply attached to his mother, while very remote from his father. He had been a boarder at his preparatory school, and afterwards at Lancing College in Sussex, and his holidays were mostly spent with relatives. At Lancing, where he was 'immensely happy', he formed romantic, though it seems chaste, friendships with boys, in particular Peter Burra. Pears was handsome and had a patrician charm. After a year studying music at Oxford he failed his preliminary examinations and took up teaching. In 1934, encouraged by Burra's sister Nell, he tried for and won an operatic scholarship to the Royal College of Music, just at the time Britten left it. He soon left the RCM too, dissatisfied with the tuition there, and joined the BBC Singers. His voice was still quite small, and he was uncertain whether he was a tenor or a baritone. His life up till now had been unfocused and dilettantish, and had he not met Britten it is highly unlikely he would have transformed himself into the extraordinary singer he was to become. Britten's first diary entries on his new friend spell his name 'Piers' – a nice Freudian slip. He refers to him as *a dear* – the same term he had used for Berkeley and Burra, but it would be several years before their relationship would go any further than close friendship. Britten's continued reluctance at this crucial time in his life to enter into any sexual relationship is very understandable. He may have been moving in homosexual circles, but it has to be remembered that homosexuality was illegal in Britain in the 1930s and punishable by imprisonment, and it remained so for many years afterwards; the Wolfenden Report in 1957 recommended decriminalization but the law was not changed until 1967. Britten himself was interviewed by the police as late as 1954 (no action was taken). Looking back from our more liberal times, it is hard to imagine the full extent of fear and guilt that homosexuals could be made to feel, especially a highly sensitive and conscientious young man such as Britten.

As his new friendship developed, Britten was continuing to collaborate with Auden, for whose play *The Ascent of F6* (again written jointly with Isherwood) he had composed incidental music in February. Isherwood remembered Britten around this time as 'pale, boyish, indefatigable, scribbling music on his lap, then hurrying to the piano to play it'.[76] The song texts Britten set, in both 'serious' and 'popular' styles, reflect Auden's then ambivalent feelings about love, and seem to have corresponded to Britten's too. It was at this time that he wrote the letter to Henry Boys quoted on p.22 about *Das Lied von der Erde* and its evocation of *never-satisfied love*. In the song-cycle *On This Island*, which he dedicated to Isherwood, the pure, aspiring joy of the opening 'Let the florid music praise' fades into the second stanza's resigned 'O but the unloved have power'; while the second song, 'Now the leaves are falling fast', is full of anxious hesitation:

> Whispering neighbours, left and right,
> Pluck us from the real delight;
> And the active hands must freeze
> Lonely on the separate knees.

In further contrast, both 'Seascape' and 'Nocturne' sustain a mood of quiet ecstasy: the latter's vocal line gently rises and falls throughout the song, like breathing (as Donald Mitchell has noted).[77] The cycle ends ironically, undermining the stoicism of the text – almost a statement of Rilkean *Dennoch preisen,* praise in spite of all – with its jazzy roulades, but finishing with a defiant D major chord. This splendid song-cycle is one of Britten and Auden's finest collaborations.

At the end of May 1937, Boyd Neel, who had conducted the music for *Love from a Stranger*, asked Britten if he could compose a piece for his string orchestra to perform at the Salzburg Festival that August. Britten jumped at the chance, undaunted by the need for haste, and finished a 25-minute piece in just over a month. *Variations on a Theme of Frank Bridge* was his first work to become a popular classic. The reasons are clear: the piece brims over with vitality and is full of instantly memorable ideas. The titles of the ten variations clearly differentiate them as 'character pieces' – the culmination of this preoccupation. Britten also intended them to provide a rounded portrait of his teacher. He originally headed all the variations with additional titles denoting Bridge's personal characteristics: thus 'March' was headed 'His energy', 'Romanza' was 'His charm', 'Aria Italiana' was 'His humour', and so on. Bridge was greatly touched by the score's dedication – 'a tribute with affection and admiration' – writing in a letter of thanks: 'It is one of the few lovely things that has ever happened to me.'[78] The theme, preceded by an introduction which forcefully presents the notes F and B, is taken from Bridge's *Idyll no 2* for string quartet (1906), which Britten had already used for an unfinished set of piano variations he began in 1932. The intervals of a falling fifth and fourth with which it begins are present in almost all the variations: these vary widely in mood, from boyish jollity to the Mahlerian tragedy of the 'Funeral March'. The fugal finale was originally headed 'His skill', but the skill that is on spectacular display is Britten's: Bridge had been right about the value of counterpoint lessons with Ireland. In its second half the 11-part fugue combines with Bridge's theme plus a series of five more quotations from Bridge's music, including the opening theme from *The Sea* that had so struck Britten 13 years before.

Shortly after the first run-through of the Variations, Britten lunched with Walton, *so obviously the head-prefect of English music, whereas I'm the promising new boy*,[79] he recorded in his diary. They continued a somewhat uneasy friendship until Britten's death: their letters to each other are always warm and admiring, though behind his back Walton showed extreme jealousy of Britten's success. Britten was to commission the one-act opera *The Bear* for the 1967 Aldeburgh Festival, and in 1970 Walton wrote a set of orchestral variations on the theme from the slow movement of Britten's Piano Concerto.

During the race to complete the *Variations on a Theme of Frank Bridge*, Britten somehow found time to buy a house, the Old Mill at Snape, a village a few miles outside Aldeburgh. He decided to share the Mill with Lennox Berkeley, but there was much work to do on it first. Meanwhile he was sharing the Finchley Road flat with Pears – since his sister Beth had moved out to get married – and composing a large-scale piece of incidental music, *The Company of Heaven*, for a BBC religious programme about Michaelmas. One of the numbers was a setting of Emily Brontë's poem 'A thousand gleaming fires' for tenor and strings – the first music he wrote specifically for Pears's voice. In March 1938 Britten and Pears found a new flat in Earl's Court, and Britten had begun a Piano Concerto for himself to play at that year's Promenade Concerts. In April, the Mill was finally ready, and Britten moved in, amidst general fears that war was imminent following Hitler's march into Austria and his threats against Czechoslovakia. Britten brought with him a Basque refugee boy, a victim of the Spanish Civil War, whom he had rashly agreed to help for a year by giving him accommodation and employment. The arrangement did not work out, and after a fortnight Beth took the boy back to London, where he was found another home. A few weeks later Berkeley arrived from Paris with José Raffalli, and Britten went to London to entertain another old school friend, Francis Barton, with whom nothing further was to develop, despite Pears's encouragement.

After several interruptions caused by these domestic and emotional complications, the Piano Concerto was finished in early July and the full score was ready by the end of the month. Shortly before its completion, Aaron Copland, whom Britten had met at the London ISCM Festival in June, and whose *El Salón México* he had singled out as the outstanding work played there, visited the Mill. Copland was a fellow homosexual and the two felt a sympathetic comradeship. Copland played through to Britten his new school opera *The Second Hurricane*, 'singing all the parts of principals and chorus in the usual composer fashion'.[80] Britten was impressed and, in return, played his Piano Concerto to Copland.

Britten dedicated the Concerto to Berkeley. The premiere, conducted by Sir Henry Wood, took place at the Queen's Hall on 18 August, and was a great success with the public, though not with the critics nor, perhaps more seriously, with the Bridges or Marjorie Fass. The latter wrote: 'if Benjy develops some day later on, he will see the insignificance of this work as it must be to all real musicians.'[81] Nor did many others seem to discern much beneath the surface brilliance, though all acknowledged this at least. Yet, one might ask, why should anyone have demanded more? Wasn't a young virtuoso allowed to write a display piece, to show off his own playing technique and his spectacular command of the orchestra? The opening Toccata is much concerned with display: the piano writing is brilliant, the orchestration ebullient; the second theme is soon given to the whole string

Kindred spirits: Copland with Britten

body almost in the manner of Tchaikovsky or Rakhmaninov. The first and second subjects are cunningly recapitulated together (an idea that Britten first employed in his *Sinfonietta*, and would use again in his first two string quartets) and the second theme achieves a poetic apotheosis. Admittedly his critics were mostly untroubled by this opening movement; it was the rest of the Concerto they objected to. Though he was hurt, Britten must have come to accept that they were partly right, for in 1945 he replaced the original third movement, which prolonged the skittish, mildly sarcastic mood of the preceding waltz, with a gravely reflective piece called 'Impromptu', which is in fact a passacaglia. This both deepens the Concerto and makes the finale more ambivalent, with its Prokofiev-like march tune which strides through the movement and reaches a somewhat grotesque climax just before the apparent triumph of the end.

'And what about its effect on a certain person of importance?'[82] Auden wrote to Britten about the Concerto from Brussels. The 'certain person' was Wulff Scherchen. Britten had met his father Hermann again at the ISCM Festival and had learned that Wulff, who was now 18, was living in Cambridge with his mother. Britten wrote to Wulff on 25 June: *I don't know if you will remember me or not . . . I should very much like to see you again.*[83] Wulff replied immediately and enthusiastically, and Britten invited him for a weekend at the Mill. Britten had by now given up writing his daily diary, so we cannot follow the progress of their friendship there, but in numerous letters – for this was a relationship quickened by absence – they give expression to new and intense emotions. Britten was surrounded by devotion: Peter Pears was probably now himself in love with him and Lennox Berkeley certainly was. Around Christmas 1938 Berkeley sent several anguished letters to Britten confessing 'mean and horrible jealousy',[84] to which Britten responded with deliberate detachment in a New Year letter: *I'm sure you're feeling fine now that you're in Paris*

with José & all those friends of yours . . . Much love, my dear; cheer up.[85]
Meanwhile Wulff's friendship with Pears was also evolving. He recalled later: 'to me Peter was a father figure, and I thought in a sense that he was the father to Benjamin at the same time . . . He had this air of stability that Ben didn't have. I mean Ben was ebullient, outgoing, and Peter was the quiet, steadying influence.'[86]

Did Wulff even at this time have a sense of what was eventually to happen? At the height of the relationship, when both of them wrote of being 'lost to the world'[87] – a Mahlerian reference – Britten was already thinking about leaving England for America. The idea may have begun with Pears's tour of the USA with the New English Singers in October 1937. Copland's visit to Snape had helped encourage it, and the realization of the idea was undoubtedly hastened by Auden and Isherwood's departure for New York in January – neither of them was to return, and Britten must have been bereft by the loss of these sustaining friendships. Montagu Slater (a left-wing writer for whose play *Stay Down Miner* Britten had written incidental music) and his wife Enid gave him a collection of American folk songs and ballads; Britten wrote in his letter of thanks: *I am now definitely into my 'American' period, & nothing can stop me.*[88] In February, Britten saw a Hollywood producer with a view to writing a score for a film about King Arthur: he was excited, and though ultimately nothing came of it the project was kept alive for several months. He himself said in an interview in 1960 that he had *felt Europe was more or less finished,*[89] and that his future lay in America. Meanwhile, as well as composing *Ballad of Heroes*, his tribute to the British members of the International Brigade who had fallen in the Spanish Civil War, which included a setting of Auden's 'Danse Macabre' (the draft took him only five days), he wrote some other music which is directly related to the inspiration this new relationship had brought him and the feelings it aroused.

Some months previously, Auden had introduced him to Arthur Rimbaud's poetry, which greatly excited him, and in March 1939 he set two poems from *Les Illuminations*, the extraordinary sequence that Rimbaud wrote as a teenager, mostly in London when he was living out his stormy relationship with Verlaine. The two songs were 'Being Beauteous' (eventually dedicated to Peter Pears) and 'Marine'. He wrote them for Sophie Wyss, still his first choice of singer, and they were broadcast, as part of an all-Britten

Young Apollo: Wulff Scherchen

concert, a week before he and Pears set off for Canada on 29 April. After a farewell party, at which Wulff was ill at ease – 'I really felt I didn't fit into this crowd',[90] he said much later – Britten saw him to Liverpool Street to catch the last train to Cambridge. They were not to meet again for over three years.

At Southampton, before Britten and Pears boarded the liner *Ausonia*, the Bridges unexpectedly appeared to see them off, and Frank gave Ben his viola as a parting gift. Britten was never to see Bridge again; he died two years later. On the voyage, Britten wrote to Copland: *A thousand reasons – mostly 'problems' – have brought me away . . . I got heavily tied up in a certain direction, which is partly why I'm crossing the ocean!*[91] Yet it was Wulff's photograph that was on his cabin table.

America Is What You Choose to Make It

Britten and Pears arrived in Quebec on 9 May 1939, and the next day reached Montreal. After two days in the city they moved up country to the Gray Rocks Inn at St Jovite, where they stayed for the next few weeks in a *log cabin at the side of a hill overlooking a grand lake & lots of forest*.[92] As soon as he had got some incidental music for the BBC out of the way (for T H White's *The Sword in the Stone*, a favourite book of his), Britten worked on his Violin Concerto, another piece he had begun in England, for the Spanish violinist Antonio Brosa.

As usual, he worked very quickly, unhampered by anything except mosquitoes (*31 bites on one foot alone!*[93] he reported to Enid Slater). By the middle of June he had almost finished the Concerto and wrote to his publisher Ralph Hawkes: *So far it is without question my best piece. It is rather serious, I'm afraid – but it's*

Antonio Brosa (1894–1979) was born in Barcelona. He settled in England in 1914 and was one of the first violinists to make radio broadcasts (from 1920). In 1925 he founded the Brosa Quartet and, after he went to the USA in 1940, he became leader of the Pro Arte Quartet. Through his friendship with Frank Bridge, Brosa met Britten in 1931 – he records in his diary for 19 March: *Go with Mummy . . . to a topping recital by Antonio* Brosa. *He is simply superb. Incredible technique, with beautiful interpretation.* The two of them gave the first complete performance of Britten's Suite for violin and piano in 1936. As we can hear from the recording he made of the Britten Concerto some time in the 1950s, Brosa played with superb, contained passion and possessed a fantastic technique, and Britten's solo part made great demands on it. Brosa played on the 'Vesuvius' Stradivari of 1727.

got some tunes in it![94] The Concerto is certainly 'serious': it confirms the mature Britten's essentially tragic vision of the world, first announced in *Our Hunting Fathers*. Both melody and accompaniment at the opening have a distinctive Spanish character, and according to Brosa, the events of the Spanish Civil War cast a dark shadow on the music. There is also much of Mahler in it, and it is appropriate that Britten should have dedicated the Concerto to his fellow Mahlerian Henry Boys. Tragedy is never far away, either in the elegiac falling melody of the first movement, or the aggressive energy of the scherzo; but it is in the finale that it comes especially to the fore, as the trombones, making their first entrance in the work, gravely announce the passacaglia theme. This was the first of his works to include this form of variations over a ground bass, of which there would be many later examples: Britten would not have forgotten the huge effect that the passacaglia finale of Brahms's Fourth Symphony had made on him as a teenager. The movement eventually attains a climax in D major, the key that throughout has been the Concerto's ideal goal; but it cannot be sustained, and the coda, which becomes more and more eloquent, vacillates between major and minor, the orchestra eventually settling on the open fifth D-A while the soloist plays an F-G flat trill: a profound ambiguity.

Living together in these idyllic surroundings, and given Pears's already strong inclination, the inevitable happened: the two friends became lovers. A change that Pears remembered as significant occurred when they visited Toronto in early June to give a joint recital. A few days later they crossed into the USA and stayed with some acquaintances of Pears in Grand Rapids, Michigan. It was here, it seems, that they consummated their love: 'I shall never forget a certain night in Grand Rapids',[95] Pears wrote to Britten six months later. And yet, at exactly this time, Britten was writing to Wulff: *It is awful how much you mean to me – I had terrific resolutions when I left – & I renew these resolutions every* day (*you* know what these resolutions are!*) – but I simply can't help thinking of you & what you're doing, & I can't bear it if your photo isn't grinning at me from the mantelpiece! I love you more everyday – and seeing all these people can't put you out of my head. So there! There's a declaration.*[96] Pears, rather extraordinarily, added a flippant post-script to this letter: 'I am looking after Ben as well as he deserves, and am trying hard to keep him from breaking out, but the Canadian girls are terribly attractive!' Britten's declaration, how-ever, was a safe one, for at present he had no intention of going back to England. *I'm thinking hard about the future*, he wrote to Wulff ten days later. *This may be the Country. There's so much that is unknown about it – & it is tremendously large & beautiful. And it is enterprising & vital.*[97]

Most likely the truth was that, for the time being, Wulff was his muse but Peter was reality: the kind of situation that is often rewarding for an artist. Britten would frequently need such a muse; but Peter, true to his name – and as Britten acknowledged – was the rock on whom he was to rely for the rest of his life and Peter's support never wavered. *Peter sends his love, & says he's look-ing after me – as he certainly is – like a mother hen! He's a darling,*[98] Britten told Wulff a few months later.

After a short visit to New York, which Britten found exciting but bewildering, he and Pears spent the rest of the summer in Woodstock, NY, renting a studio near Copland's house there. Many years later Copland recalled their games of tennis, which Britten always won (he was a brutally competitive player). At Woodstock Britten wrote some music quite different in tone from the Violin Concerto: two more Rimbaud songs, including 'Antique', dedicated to Wulff, and a 'fanfare' for piano and strings in a radiant A major which owed much to his new experience of American sunlight, but was also inspired by Wulff. This was *Young Apollo*, commissioned by the Canadian Broadcasting Corporation for himself to play. The title came from the last lines

Britten, Copland, Pears: New York State, Summer 1939

of Keats's unfinished *Hyperion* with its evocation of Apollo's 'golden tresses' and 'limbs celestial'. The thematic material is almost entirely based on scales and arpeggios, as in *Les Illuminations*. Why, after two performances, did Britten withdraw it? It was not played again in his lifetime: was this for musical or personal reasons?

In August the two of them moved again, to Amityville, Long Island, to stay with the Mayers, an immigrant German family Pears had befriended on his earlier visits to the USA. Elizabeth Mayer and her psychiatrist husband William lived with their four children in a house in the grounds of Long Island Home, the mental hospital where Dr Mayer worked. Mrs Mayer soon became enormously fond of Britten and almost a second mother to him. In a letter to Enid Slater, Britten described her as *one of those grand people who have been essential through the ages for the production of art; really sympathetic & enthusiastic, with instinctive good taste (in all the arts) & a great friend of thousands of those poor fish – artists. She is never happy unless she has them all around her . . . I think she's one of the few really good people in the world – & I find her essential in these times when one has rather lost faith in human nature.*[99] The original plan had been for Pears, at least, to return at the end of the summer, and he booked a passage on the *Queen Mary*. Britten persuaded him to

Britten and Pears with the Mayers

stay, however, and when war broke out on 3 September, the wisdom of this decision was confirmed. Britten had seen Auden again: the two of them were planning an operetta for children which would eventually become *Paul Bunyan*. Britten's own pacifism had been strengthened by talking to his old friend who, in the euphoric state of his own discovery of love (for Chester Kallman) was soon to write his poem 'September 1, 1939' with its famous line 'We must love one another or die' (which later, disillusioned by Kallman's betrayal of his trust, he would repudiate).

In Amityville Britten also met Colin McPhee, who introduced him to the music of Bali, where McPhee had lived for a number of years.[100] This contact with Balinese music was eventually to have far-reaching results, beginning with a hint of gamelan music at the point in the opening scene of *Paul Bunyan* where the moon turns blue. Britten straight away got down to work and after finishing a sketch of *A.M.D.G.*, settings of poems by Gerard Manley Hopkins initially intended for Pears's madrigal group the Round Table Singers, but which he then abandoned for unknown reasons, he turned to the completion of *Les Illuminations*. On 19 October, just after he had finished the song-cycle, he wrote to Sophie Wyss: *Les Illuminations, as I see it, are the visions of heaven that were allowed the poet, and I hope the composer.*[101] The visions are very direct: Christopher Palmer has pointed out that only a 'naive' composer, in Schiller's sense of the word, would have dared set these poems so simply.[102] The marvellous opening, with its high trill for cellos and basses and trumpet-like fanfares for violas and violins in B flat and E major, leading to the soloist's 'J'ai seul la clef de cette parade sauvage' ('I alone hold the key to this wild parade'), heralds the amazing variety of vivid scenes that follow. The kaleidoscopic dash through the cityscape of 'Villes' succeeds to the still, sensuous love poetry of 'Phrase' and 'Antique' (so much more sensuous when sung by the soprano

Relaxing: Britten and Colin McPhee, Stanton College, 1941

voice for which the songs were conceived); the brilliance of 'Royauté' and 'Marine' to the rapt 'Interlude' and the loveliest song of all, 'Being Beauteous', which glides effortlessly in and out of the purest C major. 'Parade', which follows, *is a picture of the underworld. It should be made to sound creepy, evil, dirty (apologies!), and really desperate.*[103] Does beauty already inevitably lead 'to the abyss', as *Death in Venice* was later to suggest? Yet this vision ends in the ecstasy of C major again, as the soloist exultantly shouts out the refrain. 'Départ' leaves the 'parade sauvage' with nostalgic regret, as the music winds down to silence. Almost all the melodic material of *Les Illuminations* is derived from arpeggios and scalic fragments; yet it all sounds completely fresh. It is the crowning masterpiece of these early years.

Britten found time to compose yet another piece before the end of the year: the orchestral suite *Canadian Carnival*, based on Canadian folk songs. It is a more serious piece than it appears, culminating in a disturbingly ironic setting of 'Alouette' which was surely provoked by the sadistic words of this disingenuous children's song. In January he gave the US premiere of his Piano Concerto in Chicago and shortly afterwards, exhausted by all his prolific composition as well as the emotions of the past year, he fell seriously ill with a streptococcal infection; he did not recover for six weeks. He would surely have been painfully aware that this was the illness that Mahler had died from. One of the Mayer daughters, Beata, a trained nurse, looked after him.

Recovered, he embarked upon his next project, a symphony, which was his response to a commission from the Japanese government for a piece to celebrate the 2,600th anniversary of the Imperial dynasty. It is hard to believe that Britten really imagined that the Japanese would think a *Sinfonia da Requiem*, with Christian associations and moreover dedicated to the memory of his parents, suitable for the occasion; a work whose central 'Dies Irae', a Dance of Death like many of his scherzos and here raised to a new pitch of violence, was a clear response to the war that was raging in Europe. In fact it looks like a deliberate attempt to disconcert, as *Our Hunting Fathers* had been. The Japanese commissioners were duly upset and the *Sinfonia* was rejected (Britten meanwhile had spent some of the money from his commission on a car), though it was soon taken up by John Barbirolli and the New York Philharmonic, who gave the first performance in March 1941. The opening movement, 'Lacrymosa', begins with doom-laden Ds on the timpani, recalling the first movement of Mahler's Ninth Symphony, which is in the same key. The climax of the 'Dies Irae', with dissonant 'fluttertonguing' brass and screaming glissandi, is so disruptive that it needs a special kind of calming, which the D major 'Requiem Aeternam', the movement

Britten had hoped might appease the Japanese, then provides. At its climax, the mourning theme of the 'Lacrymosa' is gloriously transfigured, with cymbal clashes suggesting the sound of the sea[104] – the symbol of ultimate peace. This was Britten's third successive orchestral work in D: one may feel that the serene ending of the *Sinfonia* lays to rest the unruly passions of the two concertos as well as its own, and also much else that had caused anxiety in the past few years of his life. For a while, his music now tells us, he was happy.

An ebullient *joie de vivre* is certainly evident in the score of *Paul Bunyan*, which occupied him for much of the next year. Auden had devised a story based on an American myth: the legendary giant Paul Bunyan (represented by an off-stage speaking voice) presides genially over a lumber camp, symbolic of progress and the taming of nature. There are Swedish lumberjacks, headed by the irascible Hel Helson; an intellectual loner, the writer Johnny Inkslinger; and an archetypal boy-girl romance between Slim, the camp cook, and Bunyan's daughter Tiny. Both Helson and Inkslinger discover themselves through their contact with Bunyan, Helson by losing a fight with him, Inkslinger by making his idealistic ambitions practical: at the end of the operetta he is offered a job in Hollywood, perhaps eventually to write *Paul Bunyan*. The story is uplifting in the spirit of Roosevelt's New Deal policies, certainly music for the people, but music that avoids compromising artistic integrity. Though it was conceived as a high school piece (with the result that some of it has high school band scoring), Auden and Britten at one point hoped *Paul Bunyan* would be produced on Broadway, as it could have been if the circumstances had been right. There is no lack of potential hit tunes: Britten's melodic gift was in full flow, and some of the songs are as catchy as those of Richard Rodgers. The cabaret songs with words by Auden that he had been occasionally writing over the past four years for Hedli Anderson served as a model, particularly for the superb 'Blues for

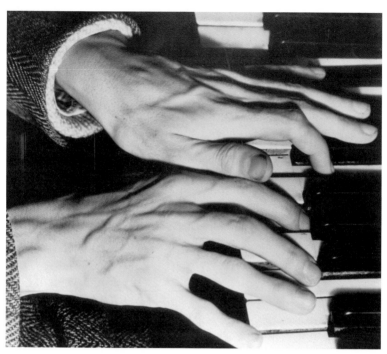

The hands of a master chamber musician

the Defeated' in Act I. Auden's libretto is somewhat self-indulgent in places – and Britten omitted the two most wayward numbers when he revised *Paul Bunyan* in 1974 – but being the work of a genius, it sparkles at times like no other libretto Britten was ever to set. It was also a work unusually free from the burden of personal guilt. In some ways it is sad that their partnership was not to continue. Britten might have learned how to control his friend's excesses, and as for Auden, neither Stravinsky nor Henze would be on the same musical wavelength for him as Britten had been.

'Once in a while, the odd thing happens, Once in a while the moon turns blue', the chorus sing near the beginning of the operetta (in E major, a key that would always have special connotations of security). *That was Peter*,[105] Britten said, when he heard *Paul Bunyan* again just before he died. During the summer of 1940 he wrote a declaration of his love for Peter in the *Seven Sonnets of Michelangelo* for tenor and piano: love here is not without its hesitations and anxieties (and there must in any case be strong contrasts in a song-cycle), but there is ardour and joy too in the expansive vocal lines, and the strength of the emotion is obvious. Meanwhile Wulff Scherchen was fading from his life: after the outbreak of the war he was interned as an alien and sent to Canada, and for a long time they had no contact. When Britten finally located him in Canada, their correspondence was censored by the authorities. He saw Wulff again after his return to England in 1942, but the relationship had inevitably changed. Wulff married some years later, and now presides over an extensive family dynasty in Australia.

By the autumn of 1940 Britten was having second thoughts about staying on with the Mayers: *one gets a bit tired of it*, he wrote to his sister Beth, *you see the Home is really a small village where everyone knows everyone & everyone's business, & the intrigues & scandals are unbelievable*.[106] They decided to take up Auden's offer of a room in a house owned by his friend George Davis in Brooklyn Heights, New York City, which was filled with a motley assortment of artists of all kinds, including the novelist Carson McCullers, the writer and composer Paul Bowles, the striptease dancer Gypsy Rose Lee, and Chester Kallman, Auden's wayward partner. Auden acted as the Paul Bunyan figure in the household, collecting rent and organizing communal meals. Conditions in the house were somewhat squalid and life was *a trifle too bohemian for my liking*,[107] Britten wrote to Beth. Nor was the atmosphere particularly conducive to work, though he continued to compose *Paul Bunyan* and completed several other works including *Diversions*, a large-scale set of variations for piano left hand and orchestra, for the pianist Paul Wittgenstein who had lost his right arm in the First World

War. *Paul Bunyan* reached the stage in May 1941. It was liked by the audience but not by most of the critics, some of whom seem to have been offended by the very idea of two clever Englishmen appropriating an American subject. Both Auden and Britten in fact thought the work needed revision. Auden would soon be unhappy with its naive idealism; Britten lost confidence in his music, though he regained it when the opera was revived in the last years of his life.

Soon after the *Paul Bunyan* performances Britten and Pears drove west to California to stay in Escondido, near San Diego, with Ethel Bartlett and Rae Robertson, a married couple and piano duo for whom Britten had already composed the *Introduction and Rondo alla Burlesca* for two pianos, and was also to write a companion piece, *Mazurka Elegiaca*, and the *Scottish Ballad* for two pianos and orchestra. He was still hoping to be asked to write a film score for Hollywood, but soon after they arrived, Britten received a commission from Elizabeth

The tennis player, summer 1941

'In the streets of New York I was young and well' (*Paul Bunyan*), Brooklyn Heights, 1940

Sprague Coolidge, the famous patron of music, for a string quartet. He eagerly set to work, composing in a shed in the garden to avoid hearing the sound of the Robertsons practising. The atmosphere became tense when Ethel Bartlett fell in love with Britten and her compliant husband offered her as a 'gift' to the embarrassed composer. The work, published as Britten's First Quartet, seems free of all this emotional turmoil. Britten's thorough knowledge of the classical quartet repertoire, and his experience of the string quartet medium since his early teens, enabled him to approach this great test of a composer's ability with huge confidence. It is yet another D major work: the overall mood is fiercely happy. The first movement's integrated slow introduction looks back to Beethoven's Opp. 127 and 132, and the energy of the Allegro is Beethovenian too, as is the spirit of the exuberant finale. The slow movement, in B flat, is a calm sea piece, anticipating (especially in its closing bars) the 'Moonlight' interlude in *Peter Grimes*.

This opera was first conceived while Britten was in California. Happening to read E M Forster's article on the 18th-century Suffolk poet George Crabbe in the BBC's magazine *The Listener*, he was straight away filled with nostalgic feelings about Suffolk. Pears found a copy of Crabbe's works in a second-hand bookshop and Britten read the poem *The Borough*, which contained the tragic story of the Aldeburgh fisherman Peter Grimes. He said later: *in a flash I realised two things: that I must write an opera, and where I belonged.*[108] His continued uncertainty about whether he should stay in America now gradually changed into a firm determination to return to England. At the end of September, following the premiere of the First Quartet, Britten and Pears made another cross-country journey by car back to the Mayers' house in Amityville. Britten dashed off a new overture for the Cleveland Orchestra, but soon afterwards he seems to have experienced a creative and emotional crisis. On a previous occasion he had told his friend David Rothman, an amateur musician who ran a hardware store at Southold (a name that would have stirred memories of Southwold in Suffolk), that he wanted to give up writing music and come and work in his store on the tip of Long Island. He said the same sort of thing now, but was also influenced by the complication of his close attachment to the Rothmans' teenage son Bobby. For a while Bobby became a muse figure and Britten wrote a folk song setting for him, 'The Trees so High', with poignant words about a girl whose father has 'tied me to a boy when you know he is too young'. The tone of the letters Britten wrote after his return to England is affectionate in an avuncular way and Bobby never realized the depth of Britten's feelings.[109] We do not know if these caused Britten anguish; maybe he had hoped that his relationship with Pears might end such infatuations. David Rothman at least was able to reassure

Auden to Britten, 31 January 1942: I have been thinking a great deal about you and your work during the past year. As you know I think you the white hope of music; for this very reason I am more critical of you than of anybody else, and I think I know something about the dangers that beset you as a man and as an artist because they are my own.

Goodness and Beauty are the results of a perfect balance between Order and Chaos, Bohemianism and Bourgeois Convention.

Bohemian chaos alone ends in a mad jumble of beautiful scraps; Bourgeois convention alone ends in large unfeeling corpses.

Every artist except the supreme masters has a bias one way or the other . . . For middle-class Englishmen like you and me, the danger is of course the second. Your attraction to thin-as-a-board juveniles, ie to the sexless and innocent, is a symptom of this. And I am certain too that it is your denial and evasion of the demands of disorder that is responsible for your attacks of ill-health, ie sickness is your substitute for the Bohemian.

Wherever you go you are and probably always will be surrounded by people who adore you, nurse you, and praise everything you do, eg Elisabeth, Peter (please show this to P to whom all this is also addressed). Up to a certain point this is fine for you, but beware. You see, Bengy dear, you are always tempted to make things too easy for yourself in this way, ie to build yourself a warm nest of love (of course when you get it, you find it a little stifling) by playing the lovable talented little boy.

If you are really to develop to your full stature, you will have, I think, to suffer, and make others suffer, in ways which are totally strange to you at present, and against every conscious value that you have; ie you will have to be able to say what you never yet have had the right to say – God, I'm a shit.

[Britten's response, sadly, is lost, as Auden threw away all letters he received after he had read them.]

him that he should continue to compose. A few weeks later Auden wrote a now famous letter in which he delineated with extraordinary precision Britten's personality as man and artist.

Britten and Pears were now waiting for exit permits and a passage on a North Atlantic convoy, 'at the height of the submarine menace',[110] as Beth Britten later put it, emphasizing that her brother had not shirked danger in voyaging back to England at that time. On 16 March 1942, four months after America had entered the war, they left New York in the Swedish cargo ship *Axel Johnson*. When they embarked, the Customs impounded the sketches of a clarinet concerto intended for Benny Goodman and a choral setting of Auden's *Hymn to St Cecilia*, imagining that these might be coded messages! Britten never went back to the concerto; he had also left the manuscript of the overture for Cleveland, unperformed, behind. The manuscript resurfaced in New York in the 1960s, but Britten at first denied it was his. When he was persuaded that it was, he wanted it destroyed; after his death it was performed as *An American Overture*. This little story seems symbolic of his definitive farewell to America and all that he had experienced there, including his relationship with Auden. For the moment, his old friend was much on Britten's mind: Auden was writing the text of a large-scale Christmas oratorio which, when finished, was certainly far too long, but Britten did not immediately reject it, as is sometimes thought: he described it to Elizabeth Mayer as *grand stuff*. He had worked closely with Auden on the *Hymn to St Cecilia* text and Auden had made many revisions to his original draft. Britten did eventually decide not to write the oratorio, but by that time *Peter Grimes* had taken over his life, and Pears's wariness of Auden's influence on Britten was helping to break up their friendship, which seems eventually to have come to a definite ending in 1953 after Britten returned a critical letter of Auden's (probably about *Gloriana*) torn into shreds.

Britten reconstructed what he had written of the *Hymn to St Cecilia* on the month-long voyage (the effortless memorability of the opening would at least have made this a simple task) and finished it. It is perhaps his finest unaccompanied choral work. The text is a resumé of Auden's advice to Britten to come to terms with himself, culminating in the superb admonitory line, 'O wear your tribulation like a rose', which rings out in one of Britten's characteristic fanfare motifs, though with a blurring of the triumphal tone on the word 'rose'. He also wrote another choral piece (*one had to alleviate the boredom!*[111] he told Elizabeth Mayer), which was also symbolic of return to England and the English choral tradition. This was *A Ceremony of Carols*, a sequence of medieval texts that Britten had found in a bookshop when the ship docked at Halifax, Nova Scotia. He set them for boys' voices and harp, and they are one of his most thoroughgoing explorations of childhood innocence; but they end in joyous acceptance of innocence lost in the final setting of 'Adam lay ibounden', with its ecstatic peals of 'Deo Gracias'. At this point in his life he could still set religious texts with apparently full conviction. And at the back of his mind as he sailed back home was the new opera, for which, just before he left, he had secured a commission for $1,000 from the Koussevitzky Foundation, and with which he would reach his full maturity.

What Harbour Shelters Peace?

Britten had been homesick, yet wartime England did not at first seem very appealing after they arrived back in Liverpool on 17 April 1942. A letter to Elizabeth Mayer notes the *drab shabiness*[112] everywhere, and the poverty of musical life in London. In May, he had to appear at a tribunal and explain his conscientious objection to war service. Under interrogation, he said that he did not believe in the divinity of Christ, *but I think his teaching is sound and his example should be followed.*[113] The tribunal's decision was that he should be called up for non-combatant duties; he objected, and his objection was accepted. Pears was also excused, and the two were able to continue their work as musicians. Pears obtained the lead part in a production of Offenbach's *The Tales of Hoffmann*, and went off on tour. Their letters to each other at this time adopt the intimate and caring tone they would always maintain. Some of their friends had been surprised to find them as a couple; in the climate of the time the relative openness of their relationship showed a defiant courage.

During the past three years there had been some hostility in the British press about Britten's absence in America, but this seems to have evaporated now that he had returned home. When Britten and Pears performed the *Michelangelo Sonnets* at the Wigmore Hall in September 1942, both audience and critics were deeply impressed by Britten's music and by the new glamour and strength of Pears's voice. The two repeated their performance in October at one of the National Gallery concerts – an important and much valued wartime institution – and recorded the work soon afterwards, their first recording together. They were soon to become one of the most famous duo partnerships of all time, whose performances of the great song-cycles such as Schubert's *Winterreise* and *Die schöne Müllerin* and Schumann's *Dichterliebe* would receive unanimous critical acclaim. Britten would also write seven works for Pears and himself to perform, in addition to his many folk song arrangements. He was hardly ever again to appear as a soloist: he now suffered too much from nerves to be able to go through the ordeal, and even in his recitals with Pears he was unable to eat before the concert, and had to drink brandy just before the performance to give himself courage.

In the audience at the National Gallery that October was Michael Tippett, who had admired Britten's music for some years. Not long afterwards, Britten was describing

Statement to the Local Tribunal for the Registration of Conscientious Objectors:

Since I believe that there is in every man the spirit of God, I cannot destroy, and feel it my duty to avoid helping to destroy as far as I am able, human life, however strongly I may disapprove of the individual's actions or thoughts. The whole of my life has been devoted to acts of creation (being by profession a composer) and I cannot take part in acts of destruction. Moreover, I feel that the fascist attitude to life can only be overcome by passive resistance. If Hitler were in power here or this country had any similar form of government, I should feel it my duty to obstruct this regime in every non-violent way possible, and by complete non-cooperation. I believe sincerely that I can help my fellow human beings best, by continuing the work I am most qualified to do by the nature of my gifts and training, i.e. the creation or propagation of music. BENJAMIN BRITTEN

Tippett to Mrs Mayer as a *great new friend Peter & I have made, an excellent composer, & most delightful & intelligent man*.[114] He came to admire Tippett more than any other of his English contemporaries, though he had reservations about the clarity of his musical thought. Imogen Holst recorded in her diary that Britten said 'he always knew what Michael was <u>feeling</u> in his music, and it moved him, but he didn't think Michael always managed to convey what he was thinking'.[115] Tippett in turn, as he wrote in his autobiography, regarded Britten as 'quite simply, the most

Michael Tippett (1905–98) was, unlike Britten, a late developer: his first notable works – the First String Quartet and the Concerto for Double String Orchestra – date from the mid 1930s. *A Child of Our Time* (1939–41) is indebted to Jungian psychology; its motto is its crucial line 'I would know my shadow and my light, so shall I at last be whole.' His opera *The Midsummer Marriage* (1946–52) is also grounded in Jungian ideas, and played as significant a role in Tippett's career as *Peter Grimes* in Britten's. Tippett went on to write four more operas, also four symphonies and five string quartets. In addition to *Boyhood's End*, he also wrote his song-cycle *The Heart's Assurance* for Britten and Pears. He dedicated his Concerto for Orchestra to Britten on his 50th birthday; in return Britten dedicated *Curlew River* to him on his 60th birthday. After Britten's death Tippett became the undisputed leading British composer.

musical person I have ever met'.[116] He showed Britten and Pears the manuscript of his oratorio *A Child of Our Time* and they promised to help him get it performed (it had its first performance in March 1944, with Pears singing the solo tenor part). Meanwhile Tippett wrote them a cantata, *Boyhood's End*, which they premiered in June 1943, after Tippett, also a conscientious objector, had gone to prison for refusing to accept his assigned non-combatant duties. After several years of self-analysis on Jungian lines, Tippett was now untroubled by his own homosexuality, and very likely tried to make Britten more confident of his. Tippett had something of Auden's intellectual authority and Britten became very close to him. As Tippett recalled, they shared a bed one night – chastely, though Pears was somewhat disturbed when he heard about it.[117]

Britten and Pears had begun to give frequent concerts for CEMA, the Council for the Encouragement of Music and the Arts (the predecessor of the Arts Council), performing the Classical and Romantic repertoire and Britten's folk song arrangements – in 1941 he had compiled the first of the four volumes he was eventually to produce. He wrote to Bobby Rothman: *We go to small villages, & play on pianos all out of tune, when some of the notes won't go down and those that do won't come up, and altogether have a pretty hectic time.*[118] Britten was also writing incidental music again for the BBC, a task that kept him busy throughout that summer. Shortly after the Wigmore Hall concert – which he told Mrs Mayer had been a great strain on his nerves, *rather like parading naked in public*[119] – he became ill with 'flu and was still not completely recovered when in March 1943 he was admitted to a fever hospital following a severe attack of measles. By this time he and Pears had bought a flat in St John's Wood, which they were to share with Erwin Stein, his wife Sophie and their daughter Marion after the Steins' flat was destroyed in 1944 by a domestic fire. Britten had also kept the Old Mill at Snape while he had been away; during his convalescence there he wrote his first real piece since *A Ceremony of Carols*, having meanwhile abandoned ideas for a Harp Concerto and a Sonata for orchestra. One of his

Tippett conducting the Leicestershire Schools Symphony Orchestra

incidental music projects in 1942 had involved the RAF Orchestra, whose principal horn was the 21-year-old Dennis Brain. Brain's seemingly effortless and utterly secure playing straight away made Britten want to write a piece for him. This was the *Serenade* for tenor, horn and strings.

The *Serenade* is a cycle of six dramatically contrasted songs by six different poets, on the unifying theme of evening and night. There are no obvious precedents for such a scheme: song-cycles in the past had always been based on a single poet, or at most two, as in *Das Lied von der Erde*. The horn's 'Prologue' uses the notes of the harmonic series, the only notes straightforwardly available on the old natural horn, and is like a Mahlerian *Naturlaut*, a 'sound of nature'. The first two songs, Cotton's 'The day's grown old' and Tennyson's 'The splendour falls on castle walls', are suffused with evening light, soft and subdued in the first song, radiant in the second. The diatonicism of these songs gives way to a tortuously chromatic melodic line in Blake's 'Elegy', whose climactic words about 'dark, secret love' cannot help but sound chillingly personal.

The Sick Rose

O Rose, thou art sick!
The invisible worm
That flies in the night,
In the howling storm,

Has found out thy bed
Of crimson joy,
And his dark, secret love
Does thy life destroy.

The falling semitones, out of which first the horn's melody is made and then the tenor's, are repeated at the end by the horn, the second, lower note 'stopped' (muted with the hand), an eerie effect Britten would have noticed in Mahler's Ninth Symphony. These two semitones (A flat and G) become the refrain of the medieval 'Lyke-wake dirge', a grim warning of punishment for sin – 'The fire will burn thee to the bare bane' – and one of the most frightening songs ever written. Ben Jonson's 'Hymn to Diana', chaste goddess of the moon, in characteristic 'hunting' rhythms that recall Brahms's Horn Trio, Op 40, is a kind of purgation, before the final song, Keats's sonnet in praise of sleep, with its central prayer: 'Save me from curious conscience, that still lords / Its strength for darkness, burrowing like a mole', the last five words once again set to the insistent falling semitone. The strings then envelop the voice like a warm blanket, and there is a fragile final peace, before the horn's farewell – a distant repeat of the 'Prologue'. Britten rather dismissively described the songs to Mrs Mayer as *not important stuff, but quite pleasant, I think*,[120] as if wanting on some level to play down one of his most personal statements.

In all these very personal works we encounter material that threatens stability to an extreme degree. As becomes still clearer in many of the operas, Britten actively dramatized his inner life in his music as few composers could. Mahler also had this capacity, which may be partly why Britten felt so close to him. When music communicates such intense feeling, one might argue that its relation to Britten's actual life becomes superfluous. But it is perhaps just this sense of intimate connection with inner experience that allows us to feel the unease that so unnervingly invades the music, and is worked through with ruthless care towards the tentative consolation of the ending. If Britten had not himself felt this level of unease, it is hard to imagine that the piece would have its precarious 'edge', the sense of things about to fall apart yet somehow holding together. And it is the finely balanced regaining of control over threatened stability that particularly contributes to the *Serenade*'s artistic success.

During the rest of 1943 Britten wrote another string piece for Boyd Neel, a Prelude and 18-part Fugue, even more ambitious than the one in the Frank Bridge Variations. He also composed the cantata *Rejoice in the Lamb*, commissioned by the Revd Walter Hussey for the Jubilee of his church, St Matthew's, Northampton. Britten set words by Christopher Smart, a little-known 18th-century poet to whom Auden had introduced him. Smart, like

Britten at the Old Mill, Snape, 1944–5

John Clare, was cruelly confined for many years in a madhouse, but his poem *Jubilate agno* is a celebration of Creation that almost entirely transcends his personal misfortunes. Smart's childlike innocence ensured his appeal to Britten, and *Rejoice in the Lamb*, while acknowledging in its setting of the lines beginning 'For I am under the same accusation with my Saviour' the unjust persecution of an outsider, is overall one of his most joyous works. In the autumn he wrote an extensive score for a radio production of Edward Sackville West's play, *The Rescue*; and *The Ballad of Little Musgrave and Lady Barnard*, a choral piece for a friend, Richard Wood, who was imprisoned in Germany: the piece was sung by the prison-camp choir.

By the New Year of 1944 he was at last ready to begin the

composition of *Peter Grimes*. Shortly after his return to England, Britten had asked Montagu Slater to be his librettist and Slater willingly agreed. *M. has taken to Grimes like a duck to water & the opera is leaping ahead*,[121] Britten wrote to Mrs Mayer on 4 May 1942. Britten had originally asked Christopher Isherwood, who rejected the idea. He did not ask Auden, but then he knew that Auden was working on the Christmas oratorio. Britten and Pears had already worked on a dramatic scheme for the opera which was not too dissimilar from the final shape of the work. As a writer of the political 'left', Slater's inclination was to emphasize the conflict between Grimes and the oppressive Borough society, therefore portraying Grimes as a victim of society's prejudices. At the start of the opera, Grimes is cleared of any foul play by the inquest into his apprentice's death, but he knows that people still suspect him. His ideals are unachievable: he feels himself unworthy to marry the widowed schoolteacher Ellen Orford, who is in a class above him, until he becomes more prosperous – which is unlikely to happen – and thus loses his one chance of happiness, since Ellen would have accepted him as he is. He quarrels with Ellen over her concern that he is bullying his new apprentice; he strikes her, and that is effectively the end of their relationship and the beginning of the end for him. There is a landslip on the cliff outside his hut, and the boy falls to his death; it is not really Grimes's fault, but the townsfolk, who are now solidly against him, would never believe his innocence. Alone and almost mad, he is advised by Balstrode, the most decent man in the Borough, to take out his boat and commit suicide by sinking it, which he does. At the beginning of a new day, the Borough's everyday life continues.

Britten and Pears's original plan of giving Grimes a much more explicitly sadistic relationship with the new apprentice was modified, much to the opera's advantage. The boy does not speak, and is presented as little more than an extension of Grimes's will: we feel that his harsh treatment of the boy stems from his anger with

Working with Crozier on the model for the Borough, 1945

himself. Although Britten and Pears saw Grimes to some extent as a representative of their own outsider status, as pacifists (which they openly admitted) and as homosexuals (which for obvious reasons they could not mention), in making him more generally 'the man who couldn't fit in',[122] as Hans Keller called him, they divested the opera of its merely personal relevance. Grimes stands apart from the others in his self-centred inability to communicate, even with the woman he loves. It is easy, nonetheless, to identify with the Grimes of Act I: at the inquest he conducts himself with dignity, and we are inclined to believe his story; we are touched by his frail intimacy with Ellen; his monologue 'Now the Great Bear and Pleiades' reveals him to us as a visionary, even if the uncomprehending listeners in the pub think he is mad; and as he sings his great line 'What harbour shelters peace?' we devoutly hope that he will find it. In Act II, with his surly behaviour towards the new apprentice and his brutality towards Ellen, our hearts may harden, though the pathetic state of near-lunacy into which he collapses in Act III cannot but move us. It is Grimes's opera and we stay with him; none of the other characters except Ellen and Balstrode can much excite our sympathy. The townspeople are shown as ordinary human beings with ordinary faults and ordinary virtues: the men are easily aroused to become a hostile, malicious crowd; the women, with the exception of the sour widow Mrs Sedley, may be capable of compassion, as their ensemble at the centre of Act II shows, but it is not sufficient to save Grimes from destruction. *It is getting more and more an opera about the community,*[123] Britten wrote in the same letter to Mrs Mayer. In a national opera, which is what in many respects *Peter Grimes* is, the chorus will have a prominent role, as in *Boris Godunov*; here the chorus is seen as a kind of natural force, with potential destructive power (so in *Boris* too) – like the sea, which is a character in itself, and helps give the opera its epic quality. *In writing* Peter Grimes, *I wanted to express my awareness of the perpetual struggle of men and women whose livelihood depends on the sea,*[124] Britten said.

What is especially remarkable about *Peter Grimes* is that at every point Britten finds the right musical language to activate the drama. His sense of timing is impeccable, and his word-setting a model of clarity. Why is it that so few opera composers – and especially British opera composers – possess these essential abilities? Even if the first is perhaps inborn, the second at least can be learned. Britten wrote: *One of my chief aims is to try and restore to the musical setting of the English language a brilliance, freedom and vitality that have been curiously rare since the death of Purcell.*[125] In this again he succeeded. Purcell, for whom Tippett shared an equal passion, was a fairly recent influence; Britten was to make a number of Purcell realizations, which he performed with Pears.

For his choral writing and the big, complex ensembles, he turned to Verdi, the best example he could have chosen. He also learned much from Berg's *Wozzeck*, the 20th century's other great outsider-figure opera, for Act III in particular, with its on-stage dance music (some of it in 'alla Ländler' tempo) and its Expressionist language for Peter's mad scene; there are even small parallels in that both operas begin with the calling of their protagonist's name, and both protagonists die by drowning.

Peter Grimes is through-composed but clearly divided into sections, like a late Verdi opera. This was a structure that, with some variation, Britten adopted for all his subsequent operas (*Paul Bunyan* had been divided into separate 'numbers'). While rejecting an all-embracing Wagnerian leitmotif system, Britten develops motifs meaningfully over long sections of the score. For example, at the climax of his duet with Ellen in Act II, Grimes's decisive 'And God have mercy upon me', where he breaks with Ellen to stand defiantly alone, is first taken up by the Borough eavesdroppers and then becomes the theme of the Passacaglia interlude. It is inexorably repeated in the bass while first the solo viola – Britten's own instrument – muses on the suffering of the apprentice, and then the variations, increasing in momentum and ferocity, express more and more the frustration of Peter's will. The duet with Ellen also demonstrates Britten's dramatic use of tonality. The whole of the duet and the parallel church service that is heard in the background is sung over a long-sustained dominant pedal on F, building up tremendous tension which finally resolves at 'upon me' into B flat, the key in which the opera began and the one most remote from the E major of 'Now the Great Bear', Peter's most idealistic moment. Grimes's submission to the Borough here seems graphically to seal his fate.

The opera is punctuated by the series of orchestral interludes which portray the sea in its many moods, from the muted colours of the grey dawn that opens Act I, with cries of herring gulls on high violins, to the brilliant glitter of 'Sunday Morning' – an extraordinary marriage of the Coronation scene from *Boris Godunov* with the Balinese gamelan music Britten had learned from Colin McPhee, producing a wholly original orchestral sound. There is much else that is arresting: the deep E flat chords of the 'Moonlight' prelude to Act III, with the gleam on the waves picked out by flute, harp and xylophone; the foghorn, a mournful off-stage tuba; and the majestic unleashing of orchestral fury in the 'Storm' interlude and the Passacaglia. But perhaps if one had to single out a single episode in *Peter Grimes* as an example of great operatic music, it would be the quartet for the women in Act II (or strictly trio, since the two 'nieces' sing in unison). This is the moment where Ellen, Auntie (the landlady of the pub) and the 'nieces' (the pub prostitutes) combine in expressing their pity for

'What harbour shelters peace?' The first production of *Peter Grimes*, with Pears in the title role

With Serge Koussevitzky, 1942

Peter's fate and for the plight of all men, in a lulling barcarolle. The three verses each climax – significantly on the word 'sleep' – in a torrent of high, sensuous sound that evokes unlikely comparisons with *Der Rosenkavalier*. Britten had been sent a score of Strauss's opera by Ralph Hawkes while he was in hospital in March 1943 and wrote in thanks: *I am impatient to see how the old magician makes his effects! There's a hell of a lot I can learn from him!*[126] The sweetness is not straightforwardly sexual; it is more like the tender feeling a mother has for her child, which is evoked with such poignancy that we experience a moment of complete safety before we are returned, with the Passacaglia, to the cruel world of reality. This duality is at the very heart of Britten's artistic vision.

The premiere of *Peter Grimes* had originally been scheduled for Koussevitzky's Berkshire Music Festival at Tanglewood,

Massachusetts, in the summer of 1944, but the festival was suspended because of the war. Pears had joined the Sadler's Wells Opera Company in January 1943, and the directors soon heard about *Peter Grimes*; after Britten played some of the score to them they were keen to stage it, and Koussevitzky graciously agreed. Britten had originally intended Grimes to be a baritone, but Pears's new status as an opera singer enabled Britten to write the part specifically for him. The producer was Eric Crozier, a young man on the Sadler's Wells production staff who was to become very important in Britten's life; the designer, whom

Eric Crozier (1914–94) worked as a producer of plays for the infant BBC Television Service from 1936–39, before joining Sadler's Wells as a producer. During the period of his collaboration with Britten, which resulted in three opera librettos and the text for *Saint Nicolas*, he was Britten's closest friend. Crozier married the singer Nancy Evans (who created – and gave her name to – the part of Nancy in *Albert Herring*) in 1949. In 1947 Britten had written the song-cycle *A Charm of Lullabies* for her. Crozier continued to see Britten and correspond with him from time to time after their special friendship ended in the early 1950s over disagreements about the future of the Aldeburgh Festival.

Britten suggested to Crozier, was Kenneth Green, a Suffolk artist who also at this time painted the most lively of Britten's portraits. His sets were a realistic depiction of Aldeburgh.

Britten was ultimately not altogether satisfied with Slater's libretto, and Slater was reluctant to make changes: just before the score was finished Britten asked Ronald Duncan to improve the mad scene, which Duncan did, very effectively. Rehearsals began soon after the completion of the score in February 1945; the conductor was Reginald Goodall, much later to become the most eminent of British conductors of Wagner after many years when his talents were neglected. The first performance took place at the newly reopened Sadler's Wells Theatre on 7 June, a few weeks after the end of the war in Europe. It was a triumph.

'Critic' in the *New Statesman* (Summer 1945):

I can vouch for the truth of the following incidents on a single-track bus journey last Saturday. They seem almost to amount to proof that we are becoming a nation of highbrows. A friend boarded a 38 bus at Green Park, asked the conductor whether he went past Sadler's Wells. 'Yes, I should say I do,' he replied. 'I wish I could go inside instead. That will be threepence for Peter Grimes.' All the way to Rosebery Avenue, a young man sitting next to my friend whistled the Tarantella from Walton's *Façade*; it is not an easy tune to whistle and the whistler did *not* get off at Sadler's Wells. But my friend did, and as he left the bus he heard the conductor shouting at the top of a loud voice: 'Sadler's Wells! Any more for Peter Grimes, the sadistic fisherman!'

All the critics recognized that here was something very new and striking. Britten wrote to Imogen Holst, Gustav Holst's daughter and a newly acquired friend: *I think the occasion is actually a greater one than either Sadler's Wells or me, I feel. Perhaps it is an omen for English opera in the future.*[127] Britten's life was changed: from now and for the rest of his life he was to be, first and foremost, an opera composer.

Our Firm-United Souls

Despite the success of *Peter Grimes*, there had been problems with the Sadler's Wells Company. Many company members were prejudiced against 'modern' music, and Britten saw no possibility of writing another opera for them, or for Covent Garden. Shortly before the premiere of *Grimes*, Britten, Pears, Crozier and Joan Cross – who sang Ellen in the performances and who had now resigned as director of Sadler's Wells – decided that the way forward was with chamber opera, and a company of their own to perform it. As a first venture, Eric Crozier suggested the subject of the rape of Lucretia; as a schoolboy he had been much impressed by seeing André Obey's play *Le viol de Lucrèce* performed by a company of young French actors. Britten asked Ronald Duncan, for whose verse play *This Way to the Tomb* he was composing incidental music, to make an operatic version of the Obey play. Britten was not to collaborate again with Slater, who became one of the first of his 'corpses' – his friends' name for people close to him who found they were suddenly dropped, usually because they somehow fell short of the high standards Britten demanded of them. Sophie Wyss became another: Britten decided her recent performances of *Les Illuminations* were *hopelessly inefficient*[128] in comparison with Pears's – but this strange criticism of a singer whom he had previously held in high regard was almost certainly influenced by his partner.

In July 1945 he visited Germany with the violinist Yehudi Menuhin to give recitals to concentration camp survivors. They went to Belsen: Britten was so shocked that he never talked about the experience, except that at the end of his life he told Pears that it 'had coloured everything he had written subsequently'.[129] It certainly

Britten with Yehudi Menuhin, 1945

affected the mood of the song-cycle *The Holy Sonnets of John Donne*, which he began on his return. Donne's dark, questioning poems are set by Britten with restless intensity. At times the musical language is almost atonal, as in 'What if this present'. But the last of the nine songs, and the finest, 'Death be not proud', offers some release, proceeding with solemn dignity over its ground bass and, on the final 'death, thou shalt die', reaching out to a proudly assertive B major chord. The songs' feverish mood may also stem from the fact that Britten had been ill while writing them. His fever had subsided by the time he began his Second String Quartet shortly afterwards. This is a larger and more contemplative work than the First Quartet, to which it stands in a similar relation as do Beethoven's 'Razumovsky' Quartets to his Opus 18 set. All three movements are in C: the outer ones in the major and the scherzo in C minor. The first movement uses sonata form in a typically inventive way, introducing three themes, each of which begins with the interval of a rising tenth, developing them within an eerie nocturnal atmosphere reminiscent of the 'Tenebroso' of Berg's *Lyric Suite*, and recapitulating all three simultaneously. The headlong scherzo, with muted strings, is dark and anxious. The finale is a passacaglia, appropriately enough for a quartet composed to celebrate the 250th anniversary of the death of Purcell, for whom the passacaglia or chaconne was a favourite form. Britten gave the movement the Purcellian title 'Chacony'. It was the largest passacaglia he was to write and its intense lyrical counterpoint makes an interesting comparison with Tippett's fugal Third Quartet written much at the same time. The last of the 21 variations ends with 23 affirmations of the tonic chord of C major, paralleling the 23-bar C major coda of the first movement (Berg was obsessed with the number 23 and often encoded it in his scores: could this have been a deliberate reference by Britten?) The premiere, by the Zorian Quartet (who had also premiered the Tippett Third Quartet), took place at the Wigmore Hall on Purcell's birthday, 21 November and the day before Britten's own – he was 32. Britten was pleased with the Quartet, writing to Mary Behrend, its commissioner and dedicatee: *to my mind it is the greatest advance I have yet made, & altho' it is far from perfect, it has given me encouragement to continue on new lines.*[130]

There was still another piece to come in this momentous year, music for a film made for schoolchildren about the instruments of the orchestra, which he wrote in less than two weeks in the second half of December. *The Young Person's Guide to the Orchestra*, as Britten called his piece, is a set of variations and a fugue on a theme by Purcell, a brilliant educational exercise – for Britten knew exactly how to demonstrate the individual character of each instrument – and display of musical skill, with the most extravagantly jubilant of all his endings. It has become his most widely played and popular piece.

At the start of 1946 Britten was ready to begin the composition of *The Rape of Lucretia*. On 24 January he wrote to Pears: *Well – I've taken the plunge and old Lucretia is now on the way . . . I think it'll be alright but I always have cold feet at this point. It is loathesome starting pieces – I always regret that I'm not a coal heaver or bus-driver and not have to depend on things you can't control.*[131] Here again he was writing an opera in which the protagonist commits suicide. The story can be simply told: the Etruscan prince Tarquinius, encamped outside Rome, is drinking with his fellow generals Junius and Collatinus. Spurred on by talk about the faithlessness of all the officers' wives except Collatinus' wife Lucretia, Tarquinius rides to Rome, boasting that he will test her fidelity. He asks for hospitality at her house, and during the night he rapes her. The next morning, Collatinus arrives and Lucretia confesses to him; he forgives her but she, full of shame and guilt, stabs herself.

A feature of Obey's play had been the inclusion of narrators who comment on the story. Britten and Duncan expanded the idea: a Male and Female Chorus (sung in the original production by Peter Pears and Joan Cross) are present on stage throughout. They set the scene, interpose their (unheeded) advice and, above all, they place the pagan tragedy within a Christian context of forgiveness. The Christian aspect Britten and Duncan gave to *Lucretia* has come in for justifiable criticism, since it can easily seem like pious moralizing after the event. In any case Christianity's profound silence about sex means that it cannot solve the real moral dilemma of the opera, which is whether or not Lucretia acquiesces in her rape. There is no obvious sign of this in her terrified protests against Tarquinius' intrusion into her bed, yet both libretto and music disclose more ambivalent feelings. Lucretia confesses that 'In the forest of my dreams / You have always been the Tiger', and Tarquinius claims 'Yet the linnet in your eyes / Lifts with desire / And the cherries of your lips / Are wet with wanting'; the music at this point does not give the lie to his observation. The whole of this scene is superbly handled by Britten and is full of the wildness, fervour and confusion of sexual desire. When Lucretia makes her confession to Collatinus, fragments of Tarquinius' music appear lightly in the orchestra as if to suggest that her memories are not as terrifying as she presents them. Collatinus' offer of forgiveness is so complete that we feel Lucretia cannot but accept it, yet she stabs herself. She cannot bear the thought that she might have unwontedly aroused in herself some deeper, darker level of sexuality. The passacaglia ensemble that follows her death ('Is it all? . . . It is all!') and its concluding quiet attempt at reassurance ('It is not all . . .') do not solve our uneasiness about Lucretia. Britten and Duncan were brave in asking disturbing questions about sexuality, but these are so challenging that what may easily seem like Christian platitudes are inadequate to answer them.

Britten exploits to the full the sonorities he can obtain from his 12 players – five winds, five strings, percussion, harp, plus a piano played by the conductor for the recitatives. The prominent harp part could be used as a textbook on how to write for the instrument, likewise the double bass. There is more use of leitmotifs than in *Peter Grimes*: Lucretia in particular has her own much repeated motif. But this is also much more an opera of set piece and recitative than *Grimes*, and Britten had learned much – and would learn more – from Mozart's recitatives with their unsurpassed skill in rapid word-setting. The tone of the music can seem a little detached at first, as if Britten is not fully involved with the story – and indeed the laddish sexual bragging of Tarquinius and Junius seems rather distant from his own sensibility. He is more at ease in Scene 2 with the women's placid life of spinning and folding linen. The music here is ravishingly beautiful: like the women's ensemble in *Peter Grimes* it evokes the protective maternal world of childhood in the sensuous yet innocently pure sound of intertwining female voices. But this is also a cloying world,

John Piper (1903–92) began as an abstract painter and an art critic. In 1935 he became art editor of the avant-garde magazine *Axis*, whose editor, Myfanwy Evans (1911–97), the 'Ringleader, tom-boy, and chum to the weak'[132] of John Betjeman's poem about her, he married in 1937. Both Pipers were associated with the Group Theatre and met Britten around this time. Myfanwy Piper was to write the librettos for *The Turn of the Screw*, *Owen Wingrave* and *Death in Venice*, and John Piper designed the sets for all Britten's operas from *The Rape of Lucretia* to *Death in Venice*. John Piper's later paintings are naturalistic landscapes, often topographical. He also became increasingly involved in stage design, with book illustration, photography (he edited and illustrated the Shell Guides to British counties) and stained glass – for instance at Llandaff and Coventry Cathedrals. After Britten's death he designed the memorial stained-glass windows in Aldeburgh Church, based on the three church parables.

from which Lucretia would need to escape were she ever to find her true self. She can do this only in death, willingly letting her dark secret love destroy her life.

The original plan had been to perform *Lucretia* at Dartington Hall in Devon, the home of the Elmhirsts, a philanthropic couple who had given accommodation to many refugee artists during the war. But Crozier happened to meet Rudolf Bing, one of the managers of Glyndebourne Opera, which was about to reopen following its wartime closure. Bing introduced him to John Christie, the eccentrically idealistic proprietor of the opera house, and Christie agreed to set up a Glyndebourne English Opera Company which would perform Britten's new operas during the summer season and then take them on tour. The Company moved down to Sussex and rehearsals of *Lucretia* began in June, while Britten finished the scoring at his usual superhuman pace (somehow he also found time to go to Switzerland for performances of *Peter Grimes*).

At first all went well, though growing tensions developed between Britten and Crozier on the one hand and Christie and Bing on the other, and Christie appeared not to care much for the music. Crozier had brought in John Piper to design the sets and costumes. Ernest Ansermet was the conductor, and Lucretia was sung by the 34-year-old Kathleen Ferrier, who had no experience as an opera singer, but possessed the most moving mezzo-soprano voice of her generation.

The premiere took place on 12 July 1946. Reviews were more mixed than for *Grimes*, and the libretto in particular came in for criticism, especially the Christian epilogue. This had been Britten's idea and he was prepared to

Pears squiring Kathleen Ferrier around Edinburgh Castle

defend it: in a letter to Imogen Holst soon after the premiere he wrote: *I've discovered that being simple & considering things spiritual of importance, produces reactions nearly as violent as the Sacre did! I have never felt so strongly that what we've done is in the right direction and that the faded 'intellectuals' are dangerously wrong.*[133] Tippett, however, who had gone to see the opera with Walton, in his forthright manner told Britten, whom he knew was next intending to write a comic opera, 'For Christ's sake don't use this librettist.'[134] He also wrote Britten a long and complex letter setting out some of his reservations about the high poetic style of the libretto, which concluded: 'the most striking thing lacking in English librettos is the knowledge of how to present emotions & characters in terms of dramatic situation & gesture whereby the words they actually sing withdraw a bit into the background'[135] – sound advice that Tippett

Britten and Ronald Duncan (right), Glyndebourne, 1946

can hardly be said to have followed himself in his later operas, at least.

Britten did not use Duncan again for any of his future operas. He was not to become a 'corpse'; their friendship continued, if rather shakily, and the composer later became extremely close to his son Roger, who was Britten's godson; but Duncan never understood why he had been rejected as a collaborator. It had seemed to him, as it had to Montagu Slater, that theirs was a good working relationship; indeed Britten was to write: *The composer and poet should at all stages be working in the closest contact, from the most preliminary stages right up to the first night. It was thus in the case of 'The Rape of Lucretia'.*[136] After *Lucretia*, Duncan and Britten had been working on an adaptation of Jane Austen's *Mansfield Park*; but without telling Duncan, Britten turned to Crozier for another idea. 'I suggested a comic opera based on Maupassant's short story,

Le Rosier de Madame Husson ['Madame Husson's May-King']'
Crozier wrote. 'Britten liked the idea, especially when he saw how
easily the action could be translated from Maupassant's France to
his own native coast of East Suffolk.'[137] Lowestoft's chief export
supplied a name for the hero, and the opera: *Albert Herring*. In the
meantime the tour of *Lucretia* around provincial cities played to
half-empty houses and lost a great deal of money, with the result
that John Christie withdrew his financial support from the company, though he was already committed to staging a new opera in
1947. The company re-formed to become the English Opera
Group (EOG), with Britten, Crozier and John Piper as artistic
directors. During the *Lucretia* tour, Britten had gone to
Tanglewood for the delayed American premiere of *Peter Grimes*,
performed by students and conducted by the 27-year-old Leonard
Bernstein. Auden, who had come from New York to see it, said:
'The performance was terrible but the work made an impression
all the same.'[138] This was one of the last occasions when Britten
and Auden were to spend any time together.

While Crozier got down to the libretto of *Albert Herring*,
Britten wrote a *Festival Overture* for the opening of the BBC Third
Programme, which he withdrew after its first performance (it has
since been revived as *Occasional Overture*). He also made orchestral
versions of five French folk songs which come close at times to the
sound world of Mahler's *Wunderhorn* songs. In December he began
the composition of the new opera, continuing it on a New Year
skiing holiday in Switzerland with Pears and Crozier; he finished
the score in April 1947. Together with his version of *The Beggar's
Opera*, *Albert Herring* is the most light-hearted and optimistic of
Britten's operas. Set in the imaginary East Suffolk village of
Loxford, it is full of references to local places. Albert Herring is
the naive and awkward greengrocer's boy, thoroughly under his
mother's thumb. The Loxford establishment, headed by the preposterous Lady Billows, choose him to be May King, since none

of the local girls is virtuous enough to be May Queen. At the ceremony, Albert is given lemonade laced with rum by the young lovers, Sid and Nancy, which is the key to his liberation: he decides to head off to town and enjoy himself. His disappearance causes the Loxfordians to believe he is dead, especially after his coronation wreath is found abandoned in the road; they sing a threnody for him, at the climax of which Albert reappears to tell them his tale of getting drunk and, by implication, losing his virginity. The shocked villagers withdraw, leaving Albert with Sid, Nancy and the village children to enjoy his new-found freedom from bourgeois convention.

Crozier, as the librettist, was the instigator of this scenario, where instead of succumbing to fate, a Britten hero vigorously asserts his independence and embraces life. The sheer exuberance of Britten's music shows how much he was in sympathy with the story, and that this was another liberation for him too. In particular, Albert's freeing himself from his mother's apron strings would have had strong personal resonances for Britten: the newly confident Albert's dismissive 'That'll do, Mum!' is, as Donald Mitchell has written, 'the final act of a long-running, domestic drama'.[139] Britten had a strong sense of humour, schoolboyish maybe, but genuine all the same, and the score of *Albert Herring* is full of fun. There are hilarious parodies of different musical styles for the various establishment characters, who in their fixed attitudes to life are all caricatures: Lady Billows's mock-Handelian pomposity, the teacher Miss Wordsworth's pseudo-Victorian roulades, the Gilbert and Sullivanesque orotundity of the Police Superintendent's laborious pronouncements. There are imitative sounds that rival Richard Strauss's sheep: fluttertonguing flute and muted horn and a glockenspiel for the whirring and chiming clock, Sid's wolf-whistle reproduced by violin harmonics, a tenor drum crack with harp and string harmonic glissandi for the swoosh of flame as Albert lights the gas. When Sid and Nancy lace the lemonade, viola (significantly Britten's own instrument) and piano play the opening of *Tristan*; and when Albert drinks we hear the full *Tristan* sound, with tremolo strings and plangent oboe. There is another sly quotation: just before the Superintendent mentions the word 'rape' in the scene before the general threnody the orchestra plays the Lucretia motif. Britten uses exactly the same chamber orchestra as for *Lucretia*, with still greater ease and virtuosity. There is more freedom too in the recitatives, which are sometimes very complex, with several 'cadenza' recitatives for almost the whole cast. Most of the score moves at lightning pace, but there are two extended passages of slow music: the second scene of Act II, a nocturne, which contains an exquisitely tender love scene for Sid and Nancy; and the magnificent threnody in Act III, another passacaglia, a complement to the one in *Lucretia*, in which general mourning alternates with each character's individual reflections on the situation in their personal musical style. The note of seriousness here especially raises this most deft of comic operas to a higher level.

The premiere of *Albert Herring* on 20 June 1947 was a great success with the Glyndebourne audience, though as usual some of the critics could not resist carping. Britten himself conducted. He never enjoyed conducting, but reluctantly came to accept that he was in fact the best interpreter of his own music. After Glyndebourne, the English Opera Group took *Albert Herring* to the Holland Festival and then performed it in Lucerne, together with *Lucretia*. It was while they were on this cumbersome and expensive tour that Pears suggested that it might be easier to start their own modest festival in Aldeburgh to perform operas and concerts with their friends. During the summer Britten had decided to move from Snape to Aldeburgh, and had bought Crag House, a pink house with a walled garden, its frontage appropriately on Crabbe Street, and with a fine view eastwards out over the sea from his first-floor study.

Aldeburgh has its own unique character. It extends for half a mile, from marshes to the north down to the Alde estuary, which at the town's southern end winds in from Snape to follow the shoreline for several miles before finally reaching the sea below Orford. At each end of the town are substantial Victorian hotels; however, Aldeburgh is not a resort, but a fishing town – there are fishermen's huts and boats drawn up on the shingle beach – and a place to retire to. Along the sea front is a narrow road for pedestrians, Crag Path, with mostly small Victorian houses and the medieval Moot Hall right by the beach, looking in danger of being swept out to sea. Behind are two more parallel streets, the second a busy High Street, at whose top end a road leads up a hill to the large Parish Church. Britten made his main home in this small town for the remainder of his life.

The first piece Britten wrote at No 4 Crabbe Street, as he wanted the house to be known, was his Canticle I, 'My Beloved

Britten and Pears buying vegetables from Jonathan Baggott, High Street, Aldeburgh, 1948

is Mine', a setting of the 17th-century English poet Francis Quarles's 'A Divine Rapture' for tenor and piano which he wrote for a memorial concert for the Revd Dick Sheppard, one of the founders of the Peace Pledge Union. It is one of his most serene works, a rededication of his love for Peter Pears, and it ends in a mood of untroubled happiness that would soon become rare in Britten's music. But not yet: for a year at least his music would continue in the blithe spirit that *Albert Herring* had engendered. His next piece was the cantata *Saint Nicolas*, written for the centenary of Lancing College, Pears's old school in Sussex. Crozier devised a libretto on the life and miracles of the 4th-century bishop who was the patron saint of the school, as well as of children, seamen and prostitutes. It is superbly conceived for the occasion, and Britten makes dramatic use of the available space, with voices sounding from the gallery. There are testing but rewarding parts for the amateur singers and instrumentalists; congregational hymns, and one of the catchiest of his tunes for 'The Birth of Nicolas'. The potential problem of an explicitly Christian and moralizing work written without full conviction (for although Britten retained much sympathy for the Church, he did not have the kind of fervent religious faith that Messiaen, for example, possessed) is not the same here as in *Lucretia*, because there is no conflict with the subject matter. All that can be said in mild criticism of *Saint Nicolas* is that there are a few places where the music seems to lack complete conviction – where it has more to do with piety than with true religious spirit.

In any case Britten was at his happiest with secular subjects. In the early months of 1948, in the midst of recitals with Pears in Italy, Switzerland and Holland, he somehow found time to write a new, almost two-hour work for the EOG: *The Beggar's Opera*. With Tyrone Guthrie, who had been the administrator of Sadler's Wells at the time of *Peter Grimes*, to edit the text and direct the production, this was by no means a simple adaptation of John

Gay's early 18th-century ballad opera, but a total recomposition, based on the original tunes but giving each a sophisticated and often highly contrapuntal treatment. *I must stop myself too much 'canonizing' of the music*,[140] Britten wrote to Pears – but we may be glad that he didn't. The story is a not untypical one for Britten, with an outsider hero, the highwayman Macheath, who has a complicated love life – he has married Polly Peachum after getting Lucy Lockit pregnant. The girls' fathers, rogues both, contrive to have Macheath imprisoned; he is about to be executed when the conventions of opera come to his rescue and all ends happily for him, if not for his two women. The music has the same quality of unforced inventiveness as Britten's folk song settings, and the scoring – the same as *Lucretia* and *Herring* – is consistently delightful. Stravinsky must surely have known *The Beggar's Opera* when he wrote *The Rake's Progress*, which seems like a deliberate attempt to outclass it, like other of Stravinsky's attempts to set Britten texts and make his own versions of existing Britten pieces: the Lyke-wake dirge in the *Cantata*; *The Flood*; *Abraham and Isaac*. Stravinsky also borrowed the 12-note row from *The Turn of the Screw* for *The Flood*,[141] and it could even be claimed that, not content with stealing Britten's subjects, Stravinsky also stole Auden for his librettist. This side of the old master is not his most attractive.

The Aldeburgh Festival had been officially constituted the previous autumn. Fidelity, the young Countess of Cranbrook, who lived nearby at Great Glemham and was a known supporter of local music, was invited to become chairman. Elizabeth Sweeting, who had lately been working for the EOG, was appointed general manager. Enough money was guaranteed for the Festival to go forward. It would centre on the Jubilee Hall, a short distance down Crabbe Street from Britten's house; the hall held just over 300 people and had adequate facilities for staging opera. The first Festival ran for a week, from 5 to 12 June 1948. There were three sold-out performances of *Albert Herring* and the unofficial premiere of *Saint Nicolas*; the Zorian Quartet played Bridge's Quartet in F sharp minor and Tippett's Second Quartet; the 21-year-old Arthur Oldham, Britten's composition pupil and amanuensis – he had copied out Britten's full scores since *Peter Grimes* – conducted his own *Variations on the Coventry Carol* for chamber ensemble. There were lectures: E M Forster spoke on *Peter Grimes* and stayed with Britten and Pears at 4 Crabbe Street; William Plomer talked about Edward Fitzgerald, the Suffolk poet-translator of Omar Khayyam; Sir Kenneth Clark lectured on 'Constable and Gainsborough as East Anglian

E M Forster (1879–1970) was, with D H Lawrence and Virginia Woolf, one of the most important British novelists of the first part of the 20th century. He was educated at King's College, Cambridge, and through close friendships made there became associated with the 'Bloomsbury Group'. It was not possible for him to publish work on specifically homosexual themes – his openly homosexual novel *Maurice*, written in 1913, did not appear until the year after his death. The novels on which his reputation is founded are *The Longest Journey* (1907), *A Room with a View* (1908), *Howards End* (1910) and especially *A Passage to India* (1922–4), one of the first books to show a sympathetic understanding of interracial relationships.

Painters', and there was an exhibition of small Constable paintings (Pears had just bought one himself, the beginning of their art collection). The Festival was a success.

Britten was busy with conducting the EOG on tour after the Festival ended, but he kept August free for a complete break. Holidays were nonetheless quite strenuous: Crozier records that Britten actually swam 'four or five times a day . . . and quite often last thing at night'.[142] Forster came to stay again, and acquiesced in Britten's request that he should collaborate with Crozier on a future opera project. Meanwhile Britten was thinking about his next large-scale piece, the *Spring Symphony*, a second commission from the Koussevitzky Foundation. This had been in his mind

Forster, Britten and Duncan on the marshes near Aldeburgh

since 1946, and he had already assembled a collection of texts to set for three soloists and chorus – both boys and adults. It was not to be a symphony in any traditional sense, though Mahler's Eighth and *Das Lied von der Erde* and Holst's First Choral Symphony can be seen as precedents. The four parts do loosely correspond to the four movements of a Classical symphony, with the slow movement second and the scherzo third. Each part except the finale is made up of a group of shorter settings, often for a solo voice, of predominantly 16th- and 17th-century poems. The choral introduction, depicting the icy grip of winter, caused Britten much trouble. He wrote to Pears on 22 October: *The work started abysmally slowly and badly & I got in a real state . . . I'm half way thro' the sketch of the 1st movement, deliberately not hurrying it, fighting every inch of the way. It is terribly hard to do, but I think shows signs of being a piece at last. It is such cold music that it is depressing to write, & I yearn for the Spring to begin, & to get on to the 3 Trumpets & Tenor solo!* Spring is heralded by the trumpets' cuckoo calls and, in the following choral setting of Nashe's 'Spring, the Sweet Spring', by the three soloists imitating cuckoo, owl and nightingale. In the slow movement and scherzo Britten gives each setting its own reduced orchestra: Vaughan's 'Waters Above' is just for tenor and violins, whose *sul ponticello* (near the bridge) patterings mimic the spring rain. Britten wrote that the slow movement was about *the darker side of Spring – the fading violets, rain and night.*[143] The finale is a setting for all the forces of a passage from Beaumont and Fletcher's play *The Knight of the Burning Pestle*. A 'cow horn' is introduced into the orchestra, insistently sounding middle C with a glissando up to the note. At the climax the boys' choir burst in with the medieval carol 'Sumer is i-cumen in'.

The *Spring Symphony* was in some ways a turning point in Britten's music. It contains his last and perhaps his finest setting of a text by Auden, the 1930s poem 'Out on the lawn I lie in bed', for which Britten creates a rapt nocturnal atmosphere, underlining the poem's central prophecy of war with muted trumpet fanfares. And the uninhibited exuberance of the ending, expressing sheer delight in life, was a tone of voice that Britten would later find hard to sustain.

On the Infinite Sea

The start of 1949 found Britten deeply depressed. He suffered from depressive symptoms all his life, but they were especially prevalent over the next few years. The causes were various: exhaustion following the completion of a work – and he probably worked harder this time than at any period of his life – as well as a recurring sense of failure, unwarranted but real nonetheless; very likely, too, the continuing painful feelings that resulted from his obsessional attractions to 'thin-as-a-board juveniles', for there had been several others since Bobby Rothman and there were to be many more. His sexuality was strong, but because of its nature and his own strong moral sense, he had to take great and sometimes damaging pains to control it.

Pears took him for his first visit to Venice, from where he sent Nancy Evans (who was newly married to Eric Crozier) a postcard of a gondolier by night which might be a scene from *Death in Venice*. On this occasion La Serenissima worked its magic and Britten returned revitalized, putting aside the scoring of the *Spring Symphony* to plunge straight into another piece about childhood innocence. Crozier and Britten devised an entertainment for the second Aldeburgh Festival called *Let's Make an Opera!* whose first half shows how the practical problems of getting an opera on the stage are solved, and the second half presents the opera itself, *The Little Sweep*, performed mainly by children. The idea for *The Little Sweep* came from Blake's poem 'The Chimney-Sweeper', later set by Britten in *Songs and Proverbs of William Blake*. Crozier introduced the opera in the Festival programme book: 'It's a very simple story about a sweep-boy called Sam. Some young children kidnap him from his ruffianly master, bath him, feed him, clothe him and keep him in hiding till he can be smuggled away to a better kind of life.'[144] The opera was very much an East Suffolk piece: it was located at Iken Hall, near Snape, and the cast were given the names of Fidelity Cranbrook's own children. There are a few places where the music verges on the twee, but they are swept aside by the vitality and charm of the conception.

Let's Make an Opera! was premiered in the Jubilee Hall, conducted by Norman Del Mar, Dennis Brain's horn-playing colleague who had taken up conducting and

'How black a gondola is – black, coffin black, (*Death in Venice*)

found it his true vocation. For the next few years, Del Mar was to be Britten's favoured conductor, until personality clashes occurred and he lost his place. Much has been written recently about the breakdown of a number of Britten's friendships and artistic associations,[145] though not so much about the enduring close friendships – for instance with John and Myfanwy Piper, Mary Potter, Imogen Holst, Marion Harewood (later Thorpe), and Kathleen and Donald Mitchell. His care for his close friends was exceptional: he invited love, which they were prepared to give him. No one questions that, like almost all artists and especially great artists, Britten was exceptionally thin-skinned and ultra-sensitive to criticism. He was also very aware that people talked about him and Pears behind his back, and when he discovered this, he felt it as a betrayal. He was capable of outbursts of furious anger. As for his working relationships, the mezzo-soprano Janet Baker, who sang in many of his works from the 1960s onwards, summed them up matter-of-factly: 'If you worked too closely with a man like him, you could face the prospect of being taken over completely. I think he was quite entitled to take what he needed from others. It might seem like ruthlessness, but success in life sometimes *requires* ruthlessness . . . From those who worked with him he demanded absolute loyalty. The commitment had to be complete. If anybody fell below his high standards, they were asking for trouble. To blame him for that is probably unfair.'[146]

The second Festival also included revivals of *Albert Herring* and *The Rape of Lucretia*, more Bridge (the String Sextet) and an exhibition of Gainsborough drawings. Del Mar conducted a concert which included the original single-strings version of Wagner's *Siegfried Idyll*, Britten's childhood after-Sunday-lunch piece. The following month, the *Spring Symphony* had its first performance at the Holland Festival. Britten was now anxious to begin his next opera. William Plomer, who had become a friend since his Aldeburgh lecture, had suggested Melville's late novella *Billy Budd, Sailor*, as a possible work for adaptation, and Britten was immediately excited by this story of the closed world of a ship at sea, and innocence destroyed within it.

Forster had not been confident enough to write a libretto alone, as he lacked theatrical experience, which Crozier possessed in abundance. They made a harmonious team, even though Forster was sometimes prickly, and criticized Britten in a way that the composer would not have tolerated from anyone else. Crozier was now living in nearby Southwold, and Forster frequently came to Aldeburgh to stay. Britten had made friends with a local fisherman, the fortuitously named Billy Burrell, who would sometimes take them out in his boat, and who also supplied fresh herrings for breakfast. In September 1951, while Britten was scoring *Billy*

Budd, Burrell took Britten and Pears, together with Basil Coleman – who was to produce *Budd* and a number of subsequent operas – and Arthur Oldham on a fishing boat up the Rhine. Robin Long, known to Burrell as 'Nipper' and a current favourite of Britten's, acted as cabin boy.

Melville's novella tells the tragic story of the handsome sailor Billy Budd, who during the Napoleonic Wars is impressed on a British warship commanded by the thoughtful, introverted Captain Vere. Billy has natural goodness and is popular with his mates, but Claggart, the Master at Arms, who is evil incarnate, determines to destroy Billy and falsely accuses him of inciting mutiny. Invited by Vere to defend himself, Billy cannot speak because of a congenital stammer – his one flaw – and instead strikes out at Claggart and kills him with a single blow to the head. A hastily summoned court sentences Billy to hang. Vere, though he admits that Claggart has been 'struck down by an angel of God', does nothing to save Billy, who goes meekly to his death. In their libretto, Forster and Crozier developed the characters of both Claggart and Vere in ways that were suggested but not fully realized by Melville. Claggart's repressed sexual desire towards Billy is spelled out more clearly than in Melville. Forster would perhaps have liked to make it still more overt, but this was impossible at the time. What Forster could say, he expressed in Claggart's great monologue 'O beauty, o handsomeness, goodness!' which Forster told Britten 'is *my* most important piece of writing'[147] (he was initially upset by the way Britten had set it). Forster makes it plain that it is Claggart's frustrated desire to possess Billy that confirms his resolve to destroy him: 'If love still lives and grows strong where I cannot enter, what hope is there in my own dark world for me?'

In the novella, Vere is a less sympathetic figure than in the opera. In Melville's account of Billy's trial, Vere persuades the reluctant officers of the drum-head court to condemn Billy – a court which, as Melville makes clear, was illegal in the first place. In the opera, Vere is loved rather than merely respected by the officers and the crew. His condemnation of Billy is seen as a necessary duty, but privately he is horrified by what he has done, ironically assuming some of Claggart's language: 'Beauty, handsomeness, goodness, it is for me to destroy you.' And before he goes to tell Billy his fate he confesses: 'I am the messenger of death . . . How can he pardon? How receive me?' In the epilogue, Vere as an old man reflects on what he did, and finds consolation: 'But he saved me, and blessed me, and the love that passeth understanding has come to me. I was lost on the infinite sea' – and he goes on, quoting from Billy's final aria – 'but I've sighted a sail in the storm, the far-shining sail, and I'm content.' For Britten, as for Forster and Crozier, Vere is the central character of the opera, and his redemption is the culmination of the drama. The Christian parallel is obvious, though not openly stated; Billy's act of loving self-sacrifice is in fact a purely human one, and may remind us of Wagner's self-sacrificing heroines. Does Vere deserve his final sense of contentment? Should Billy have so passively accepted his fate? The music seems to answer yes to both questions. The opera ends in B flat major, resolving the initial conflict with G major which dominates the Prologue, where Vere introduces the drama. Billy finds his own peace in the key of F major: following the F minor of the death sentence (the key, also, of Claggart's 'I . . . will destroy you') and Vere's subsequent aria of anguish and self-laceration, the elemental 34 triadic chords of the wordless 'interview music' gradually and very firmly establish F major, in preparation for Billy's tranquil aria of farewell in that key. We do not know what Vere said to Billy during the interview, but we know its results, since at the end of Billy's last aria, over a partial repeat of the 'interview' chords, he proclaims: 'I'm strong . . . and I'll stay strong . . . and that's enough.'

Billy Budd is, of course, an opera without women's voices, which

Crozier at first thought might be problematic, but it isn't; it is simply one of the factors – another is the spectacular orchestral use of brass and woodwind – that contribute to the opera's unique sound. And Britten's use of his male chorus in *Billy Budd* is as extensive, more elaborate and still more assured than the choral writing in *Peter Grimes*. There are four major choral scenes in the opera: the opening, with its great cries of 'O heave away, heave'; the sighting of the French frigate at the start of Act II, a tumultuously energetic ensemble that generates huge excitement; the execution scene and the ensuing near-mutiny when the crew crescendo in a terrifying wordless fugato which sounds like a vocal version of the *Peter Grimes* storm; and most memorable of all, perhaps even the supreme moment of the opera, the 'Blow to Hilo' episode at the centre of Act I. We first hear the sailors quietly singing their shanty below decks; the curtain falls and Britten takes up the melody in the orchestra, beginning gently on the strings, then in vigorous and forceful two-part counterpoint. The music dies down, swelling up again in conflicting keys as the curtain rises on the assembled sailors on deck. Their unison B flats, bursting in dissonantly onto the striving orchestral sounds, sweep into a huge, ecstatic outburst of E flat major. Everything that Britten had ever felt about the sea is expressed here. A tremendous, overwhelming sense of nostalgia is embodied in the words 'say farewell', repeated over and over again in rich canon. But unlike Delius, it is not filled with regret. It is a farewell to youth, life, love; but all in a spirit of acceptance, and an almost religious feeling for the sea as the great mother. Britten rarely revealed himself with so little inhibition and so much emotion; he was never to do so quite as powerfully again.

Billy Budd is Britten's grandest opera and in some respects his greatest. His portrayal of the evil Claggart, whose music is mostly the superbly sinister sound of trombones in parallel triads, rivals its obvious model, Iago in Verdi's *Otello*. Vere – Pears's role – is the most intriguing of his outsider heroes. The structure of the work was improved by Britten's 1960 revision which turned the original four acts into two. The original ending of Act I was excised and a new linking scene contrived; Acts III and IV could simply be joined together. The premiere of the four-act version at the Royal Opera House, Covent Garden on 1 December 1951, conducted by Britten and broadcast on the BBC Third Programme, with the young American baritone Theodor Uppman in the part of Billy, was enthusiastically received, though as usual the critics were divided. The faction fighting for him was headed by Hans Keller and Donald Mitchell, who regarded him as the foremost living composer; they would shortly publish a symposium expressing and substantiating that view.[148] Though increasingly irritated by his hostile critics, Britten was quietly confident about *Billy Budd*, telling Imogen Holst a year later that though it 'would never be a popular success he was very glad he'd written it, and to a few of his intimate friends it would always mean a great deal'.[149] He had told Marion Harewood while he was writing the opera that *I've never been so obsessed by a piece.*[150] After the first performance he wrote to thank his librettists. To Crozier he said: *I've written to E.M.F. & told him that I think you & he have produced the finest libretto I've ever heard or*

The original four-act version of *Billy Budd* has its defenders, chiefly because in omitting the last scene of Act I, a muster of the sailors who swear their allegiance to their captain, Britten made two crucial changes: he delayed the appearance of Vere until his soliloquy in his cabin, so we do not see him interacting with his crew until much later; nor do we hear Billy exclaiming 'I'll follow you, I'll serve you, I'll die for you, Starry Vere!' – words that have an ironic resonance as he goes to his death with a last 'Starry Vere, God bless you'. This scene is thus a definite loss, but since it was so clearly music for the end of an act, it had no place in the revised version; moreover Britten had always been uneasy about it, initially because one critic had compared the music to *HMS Pinafore*.

read. And I think many people realise it too.[151] Crozier, in reply, wrote 'I liked particularly the remark made by K Clark to Morgan – that "it is one of the great master-pieces that change human con-duct". Perhaps I have misquoted, but that was the gist of it.'[152]

Britten took almost two years to write the music of *Billy Budd*, interrupting it to write three pieces: the viola and piano piece *Lachrymae*, 'Reflections on a song by John Dowland' for William Primrose and himself to play at the 1950 Aldeburgh Festival; *Six Metamorphoses after Ovid* for oboe for the 1951 Festival, first per-formed by Joy Boughton from a

Theodor Uppman in the title role of *Billy Budd*, 1951

boat on nearby Thorpeness Meare and now the most widely played piece for oboe solo in the repertoire; and a realization (made jointly with Imogen Holst) of Purcell's *Dido and Aeneas*, presently ignored because of the current fashion for 'authenticity'. The pendant to *Billy Budd* was Canticle II, 'Abraham and Isaac', which Britten composed for Pears and Kathleen Ferrier in January 1952. Its opening – E flat major arpeggios ascending on the piano and the voice of God sung by the two voices in harmony together – is a stroke of pure genius, *worth a million dollars*,[153] as Tippett remembered Britten telling him. This time the sacrifice of an innocent victim is avoided, and there is rejoicing over the salva-tion of a child – a theme to which Britten could bring all his deepest feelings. Yet it is, in truth, a terrible story of a tyrant deity demanding unheeding obedience from his subjects, which

William Plomer was born in 1903 in South Africa of English parents. He lived in Japan in the late 1920s for two years before coming to London, where he wrote and published poems, novels and short stories. While working as a reader to the publisher Jonathan Cape he discovered the diary of the 19th-century clergyman Francis Kilvert, which he edited and which caused a considerable stir when it appeared in print. During the Second World War Plomer worked for Naval Intelligence. A homosexual, he became friends with Britten in the late 1940s and remained close to him until his death in 1973. His poems, particularly those from the 1930s and 1940s, cast a wryly satirical eye on the social life of his time.

Britten does not question here; later, in the *War Requiem*, he would.

In March 1952 he and Pears went on a skiing holiday in Austria with George and Marion Harewood. One day the après-ski conversation turned to national operas – *The Bartered Bride, Die Meistersinger, Boris Godunov* – and the lack of a British example (since *Peter Grimes* had not yet achieved its present emblematic status). 'Well, you'd better write one',[154] Harewood said. When they turned to a subject, Elizabeth I seemed an obvious choice and, with the Coronation of a new Queen Elizabeth imminent, Harewood agreed to do his best to organize the production of a new opera at Covent Garden in 1953 as part of the festivities. This would be based on Lytton Strachey's *Elizabeth and Essex*, which Harewood happened to have just read, and called *Gloriana*. Britten did not appear to be concerned about the tight schedule, though Pears was put out that their planned recital programme for the following year would be disrupted. Britten's first choice of a librettist was William Plomer, with whom he had already been discussing two ideas for a children's opera. If Plomer was unwilling, Britten agreed to Harewood's suggestion of Ronald Duncan. Crozier was not considered: Britten's and his close friendship had ended 'as a result of strains and tensions that were mostly on my side',[155] as Crozier later wrote. The crucial rift seems to have come about a few years later, when Crozier suddenly demanded that Britten should bring the Aldeburgh Festival to an end, an extraordinary and immediately alienating suggestion.

Plomer did agree to write *Gloriana*, and Britten soon brought in his regular set-designer John Piper. The libretto was written over the summer of 1952 so that Britten could start composing in September. There is an extensive correspondence between Britten and Plomer about *Gloriana*: Britten's letters suggesting improvements to Plomer's drafts are reminiscent, in their practical approach, of Richard Strauss's letters to Hugo von Hofmannsthal. After Plomer had sent him the opening scene, Britten replied: *Terribly good. I am delighted with it & the ideas come fast & furious. I'd like to start the tournament earlier, so, in fact, that practically the whole of it could be described by Cuffe. Could Essex have more asides – such as 'Heavens' – 'I can't bear it' kind of thing? Which leads to one general worry . . . I think that metre & rhyme (especially the latter) may make the recitatives very square, & unconversational. Can we take out a word here & there to break them up?*[156] Overall, he found Plomer a most congenial collaborator. *William is a treasure*,[157] he wrote to Basil Coleman, who was to be the opera's producer.

He decided to ask Imogen Holst to act as his assistant, to make the vocal score and prepare the full score by ruling barlines and writing in the names of the instruments. In September 1952 she began a detailed diary which she kept for the next 18 months: its tone is somewhat similar to Natalie Bauer-Lechner's *Reminiscences of Gustav Mahler*, and her relationship with Britten has much in common with Bauer-Lechner's with Mahler. In her diary, Imogen Holst gives a detailed account of the compositional process of *Gloriana* – Britten scoring so fast in the later stages that she could scarcely keep up with him. She also records many things he said, and occasionally reveals her own feelings – for she was clearly in love with him at this time. Despite some disruption when Britten's house was flooded after the severe East Coast gales at the

Imogen Holst (1907–84), the only child of Gustav Holst and his wife Isobel, at first hoped to become a professional dancer, and attended ballet classes at the Royal College of Music, where she also studied piano, composition and conducting. She composed throughout her life, but largely sacrificed her own ambitions for the sake of, first, her father's music – she wrote two important books on him and devoted much time to editing his compositions – and then Britten's. She lived in Aldeburgh from 1952 until her death, latterly in a small modernist house, and was Britten's amanuensis from 1952 until 1964. She often conducted at the Aldeburgh Festival, in particular concerts of early music and that of Purcell, for whom she had a passion that equalled Britten's own. She co-edited with Britten their versions of *Dido and Aeneas* and *The Fairy Queen*.

end of January 1953, the composition draft was finished in just over five months, and the full score, over 400 pages long, only four weeks later.

Plomer's libretto sets the private story of Elizabeth and Essex within a series of public events: a tournament, a masque, a court ball. The impetuous young Earl of Essex is the ageing Queen's favourite. Lytton Strachey describes his divided, unstable personality: 'he might have been a scholar, had he not been so spirited a nobleman . . . he ran and tilted with the sprightliest; and then suddenly health would ebb away from him, and the pale boy would lie for hours in his chamber, obscurely melancholy, with a Virgil in his hand.'[158] It might almost be a description of Britten, as he must have realized when he marked this passage in his copy of *Elizabeth and Essex*; it was fundamental to his treatment of Essex in the opera. Essex wants the Queen to make him Lord Deputy in Ireland, in order to quell a rebellion there; she is reluctant, knowing in her heart that he is not fit for the task. She finally agrees, but Essex fails; he hurries back to England and bursts into her dressing chamber to tell her. Elizabeth will support him no longer; Essex, in a panic, starts a rebellion himself, and is arraigned for treason. Against her deepest wishes, Elizabeth signs his death warrant. Duty is in conflict

Imogen Holst at work with Britten and Pears

with private feeling: it is a parallel situation to Vere's condemnation of Billy.

Gloriana has its own splendours. If it is not quite the equal of the operas that stand either side of it, this is probably because Britten was not as involved in its subject matter as he had been with *Billy Budd*, or would be with *The Turn of the Screw*. Yet the private story within the opera certainly much interested him, and the 'private' music – for instance the beautiful quartet 'Good Frances, do not weep' and Essex's second duet with the Queen – is always compelling, and becomes more so as the opera develops. As for the 'public' music, Britten was clear from the start that he was making no concessions. He told Harewood: *It's got to be serious. I don't want to do just folk dances and village green stuff.*[159] The set of Choral Dances he wrote for the masque and the Courtly Dances (Pavane, Galliard, La Volta, Coranto) for the ball scene are not pastiche, but loving re-creations of the Elizabethan style which are also always recognizably Britten's. There are other examples of this neo-Renaissance manner in the opening set of variations that accompany the tournament, and Essex's two lute songs. There is a directness in this music that is new; it was certainly intended. Donald Mitchell recalls Britten saying at an orchestral rehearsal: *You know, the more simple I try to make my music, the more difficult it becomes to perform.*[160] Much of the music that Britten wrote in the second half of his composing life (*Gloriana* comes at the mid-point) reflects this aim towards a greater simplicity, which will reach its apogee in the last works, with no loss of weight in the musical argument.

The premiere of *Gloriana* at the Royal Opera House on 8 June 1953 in front of the newly crowned Queen and various assembled dignitaries was a flop, far beyond the simple fact that the applause was somewhat muted because many of the audience were wearing gloves. The opera's failure might in any case have been expected with an audience who were probably hoping to hear something like Edward German's *Merrie England*; it highlighted the ingrained philistinism of the English establishment, for most of whom contemporary music would have meant nothing at all. The popular press characteristically used the occasion to make stupid remarks; though Britten had his defenders in the serious papers, and *Gloriana* did well at the box office, leading him to suppose that it would soon be revived. In fact after a provincial tour the following year it would not be staged again in Britain until 1966. The fiasco of the premiere did not seem overly to upset him: he must surely have been half expecting it because of the inappropriate subject he had chosen. Probably a part of him still secretly wanted to shock, as with *Our Hunting Fathers* and the *Sinfonia da Requiem*. He wrote to William Plomer: *I expect that you, like me, have felt a bit kicked around over it – perhaps more than me, because I'm a bit more used to the jungle! But the savageness of the wild beasts is always a shock.*[161] He did take one criticism on board: there was a general feeling that the Epilogue, a spoken melodrama in which Elizabeth as an old woman was confronted by a number of spectral figures, was too obscure. Britten simplified it, so that it becomes almost entirely a monologue for Elizabeth reflecting on her achievements. *Gloriana* still ends, however, with the off-stage chorus singing the madrigal 'Green leaves', fading away into silence rather like the end of Holst's *Planets*, an ending as remote from pomp and circumstance as it is possible to imagine.

When Britten agreed to write *Gloriana*, he had to postpone a commission he had already accepted for a chamber opera for the EOG to be performed in Venice. Before he turned to this, he wrote a new song-cycle for Pears and himself called *Winter Words*, settings of Thomas Hardy, a poet whose sceptical but intensely humane philosophy was in many respects close to Britten's own. The overall tone of *Winter Words* is thoughtful and often disquieting: in the longest song, 'Midnight on the Great Western', the 'journeying boy' of the subtitle is observed on a train travelling towards an unknown, lonely destination: the verses are punctuated by the mournful sound of the train's whistle, imitated by the piano. But there are also more kindly moments of vision, like the angel choir in 'The Choirmaster's Burial', and the joyous bird songs in 'Proud Songsters'. As in the John Donne cycle, everything converges on the final song, 'Before Life and After', whose first stanza encapsulates the essence of Britten's world view:

> A time there was – as one may guess
> And as, indeed, earth's testimonies tell –
> Before the birth of consciousness,
> When all went well.

Britten writes this song as a quietly passionate plea for the return of innocence to the world: the music moves steadily over pulsating triads in the bass towards its heartfelt final cry: 'Ere nescience shall be reaffirmed / How long, how long?' It is one of the key moments in his music.

The new opera was to be based on Henry James's novella *The Turn of the Screw*, which Britten first encountered in 1932, when he heard a radio dramatization and commented in his diary: *a wonderful impressive but terribly eerie & scarey play.*[162] William Plomer did not care for James, but whether that was the reason Britten chose yet another new librettist is not certain; in any case he asked Myfanwy Piper, John Piper's wife and an old friend from pre-war Group Theatre days, to adapt the novella for him. In fact she had suggested the subject to him. 'It is a curious story' is the libretto's first line – and it is; but as Myfanwy Piper guessed, absolutely right for Britten. A governess arrives at Bly, a remote East Anglian country house, to look after two children there, Miles and Flora. Their parents are dead, and their uncle and guardian, who has engaged the governess, has no contact with them. The governess imagines herself as being a second mother to the children, and at first she is charmed by them; only gradually does she discover that they are not as innocent as they seem. At the same time she sees a strange figure on a tower who, as she learns from the housekeeper, Mrs Grose, must be the ghost of Peter Quint, the master's valet. He had died not long before, as had the previous governess, Miss Jessel. The two had been lovers, and it becomes apparent that they had corrupted the children (James strongly hints that in Quint's relation to Miles the corruption was sexual) and that the children are still in their power in some way. The story becomes a battle between the governess and Quint for Miles's soul; in the end Quint admits defeat when Miles curses him, but the boy then falls dead in the governess's arms.

James's story allows both for a literal interpretation – that the ghosts are real – and a 'psychological' one – that they are figments of the governess's overheated imagination, so much so that she succeeds in frightening Miles to death. Ambiguity was certainly part of James's larger intention, which was to emphasize the atmosphere of terror and of evil, and to make the reader '*think* the evil, make him think it for himself'.[163] Ambiguity was central to Britten's vision too, but in the opera the ghosts are plainly real: they have singing roles, and there is a scene in Act I when Quint appears to Miles in the governess's absence. The first act builds towards this crucial scene: the sensual sounds of female voices and Miles's soft, sweet treble prepare us for what is one of the great seduction scenes in opera, as Quint calls to Miles in melismatic phrases that sound oriental (though their inspiration in fact was Pears singing Pérotin's motet *Beata Viscera*), and beguiles him with irresistible words: 'I'm all things strange and bold . . . I am King Midas with gold in his hand.'[164] The climax of the act, when Miss Jessel appears too, is, as Christopher Palmer remarked, as much sexual as dramatic, 'a fabulous fountain of sound'. We, too, may be seduced by this music; but in Act II we quickly learn the reality of evil, as the ghosts come together to proclaim (to a variation of Quint's melisma) 'The ceremony of innocence is drowned' – a line Myfanwy Piper took from Yeats – and their work of corruption is gradually revealed in full.

The structure of the opera is unusually tight. There are two acts, each of which contains eight short scenes; each scene is preceded by an orchestral variation, usually anticipating its mood and colour, which is based on a 12-note theme built out of fourths and fifths. Before the initial statement of the theme comes a prologue (a late addition to the score) which sets out the background to the story. As the variations proceed, there is an inexorable feeling of the screw tightening, as the opera builds towards its terrible conclusion. There is a strong contrast between the mostly diatonic and still hopeful Act I and the expressionistic chromaticism that dominates Act II, where we hear the music darken into nightmare. The first hint of something sinister occurs when a high chromatic violin line, a premonition of Quint's melisma, creeps in as the governess arrives at Bly; this later becomes associated with the celesta, Quint's particular instrument and in the opera the very embodiment of the uncanny. The music for Quint and Miss Jessel at the end of Act I, with celesta, harp and gong, has an entirely exotic feeling, prefiguring the Balinese sounds of *The Prince of the Pagodas* and *Death in Venice*. Britten had returned to the familiar chamber orchestra of *Lucretia* and *Herring*: he knew all the players of the English Opera Group orchestra personally, and was writing for them as individuals.

In October 1953 Britten developed acute bursitis, a swelling in his right shoulder, and had to cancel all engagements. He spent Christmas at Schloss Wolfsgarten near Frankfurt with Prince Ludwig of Hesse and the Rhine and his Scottish-born wife Margaret, known as 'Peg', whom he had met through the Harewoods (Prince Ludwig and Lord Harewood – a grandson of George V – were cousins). Both Hesses, Peg in particular, were to become close friends. *I've been thinking & thinking about Act I & having lots of ideas*,[165] Britten wrote to Myfanwy Piper (with his left hand), but as yet he had written no music. He did not begin composing *The Turn of the Screw* until 30 March 1954, having by then recovered the use of his right hand. He worked at tremendous speed, finishing the composition sketch on 23 July, and with the help of Imogen Holst all was ready for the first orchestral rehearsals in early August. The premiere, conducted by Britten, took place in the 18th-century Teatro la Fenice in Venice on 12 September. Jennifer Vyvyan was the governess, Quint was sung by Pears. The 12-year-old David Hemmings, who was later to become a film star, most famously in Antonioni's classic 1960s film *Blow Up*, played Miles. Britten became infatuated with David Hemmings for a while, an uncanny parallel to the role he was creating for him, as well as an anticipation of the story of *Death in Venice*. Pears found this particular obsession hard to cope with, although as usual he was tolerant and compassionate. Hemmings in adult life has seen the relationship only as rewarding for him: 'Of all the people I have worked with, I count my relationship with Ben to have been one of the finest . . . And it was never, under any circumstances, threatening . . . Did I feel that he was desperately fond of me? I suppose I did, but I must say I thought far more in a sort of fatherly fashion; and I had a very bad father-son relationship.'[166]

In April 1955, Britten wrote to Edith Sitwell about his Canticle III, 'Still falls the rain', which after he returned from Venice he composed as an epigraph to the opera: *Writing this work has helped me so much in my development as a composer. I feel with this work & the Turn of the Screw . . . that I am on the threshold of a new musical world . . . your great poem has dragged something from me that was latent there, and shown me what lies before me.*[167] He was exaggerating about Canticle III, since that piece could not have come into being without *The Turn of the Screw*, which is one of his finest masterpieces, and a work that opened up new musical landscapes for him. But he did attach great importance to the Edith Sitwell poem, whose subtitle is 'The Raids 1940, Night and Dawn', and which relates Christ's Passion to the horror of the Blitz. It is one of only two Britten works to refer directly to the Second World War. Canticle III was dedicated to the memory of Noel Mewton-Wood, a fine pianist who had performed at the Aldeburgh Festival, and a fellow homosexual who, after the death of a lover, committed suicide at the age of 31. Britten wrote to Edith Sitwell: *in its courage & light seen through horror & darkness [I] find something very right for the poor boy.*[168] The horn part was written for Dennis Brain, who was also to die tragically (in a car accident two years after the premiere). The structure of the piece is very lucid, and its language and grammar are close to *The Turn of the Screw*. Six verses for voice and piano, each beginning with the same vocal phrase in B flat for the words

'Still falls the rain', alternate with a theme and six variations for horn and piano.

Now he had another huge task ahead of him, a full-length ballet, which John Cranko, who had devised the choreography for *Gloriana*, had invited him to write for Covent Garden. But Britten was exhausted: in the past ten years he had composed eight operas, the *Spring Symphony*, *Saint Nicolas* and over a dozen smaller pieces, and he needed a rest. *Yes we <u>will</u> have a holiday next year – no more years like this in a hurry*,[169] he wrote to his sister Barbara at Christmas.

Sleep's Healing Power

In February 1955, Britten and Pears rented a villa in Zermatt in Switzerland for a few weeks' skiing. They invited Beth, Mary Potter – the painter wife of the writer Stephen Potter, whose marriage had just broken up – and Ronald Duncan and his wife Rose Marie to stay with them. On the first day, Mary Potter injured her leg, and Britten wrote an *Alpine Suite* for three recorders for her to learn to play with Pears and himself while she was recuperating.

He began writing the ballet, *The Prince of the Pagodas*, but was in no hurry to finish it. By the autumn he had sketched the first of the three acts and begun the second. On 31 October he and Pears set off on a five-month trip to the Far East, the longest journey they were ever to make. It was partly a holiday, but the two of them gave many recitals as well. Starting in Holland, they travelled across Europe to Yugoslavia, then Istanbul. They flew to India (where Britten was impressed by the sitar playing of the young Ravi Shankar), and on to Malaya, Bali, Hong Kong and Japan. During the trip Britten wrote a series of long letters, a kind of diary, to his godson Roger Duncan. He had told Ronald Duncan that he would like to become a second father to Roger: would Duncan mind?[170] Duncan made no objection, feeling that he was himself an inadequate parent. No relationship brought out the latent paternal longings in Britten more than this one. Britten had Roger to stay at Aldeburgh, visited him at school, gave him presents and wrote him several hundred letters and cards over the next ten years. In the travel diary letters, Britten gives vivid descriptions of his experiences. Driving through the jungle in Ceylon, *we saw some exciting things: lots of monkeys of course, sitting in the road & leaping through the trees, some wild cats (with long striped*

Britten and Pears arriving in New Delhi, 1955

tails), the car was charged by a large water buffalo (luckily it missed), and, finally just after it got dark a <u>LEOPARD</u> *streaked across the road in front of the car! We couldn't believe our eyes, so we stopped the car & sat waiting, and it came back onto the grass verge and watched us, for nearly two minutes, & we could see it baring its teeth at us in the lights of the car!*[171]

In Singapore they were joined by the Hesses who accompanied them for the rest of the journey. The climax of their trip was visiting Bali, where Britten at last encountered live the gamelan music that had fascinated him since first discovering it through Colin McPhee. An added attraction was that the gamelan orchestras were sometimes made up of beautiful young boys. Britten wrote to Imogen Holst: *The music is <u>fantastically</u> rich – melodically, rhythmically, texture (such orchestration!!) & above all <u>formally</u>. It is a remarkable culture . . . At last I'm beginning to catch on to the technique, but it's about as complicated as Schönberg.*[172] The experience of Bali had a profound influence on him: above all its music, but also the sensuous Hinduism he encountered there, which gave him an ideal of a religion without guilt, a possible alternative to Christianity and its obsession with sin.

Back in England, he now had to get back to work in earnest on *The Prince of the Pagodas*. He was supposed to finish by September

1956, but was able to postpone the deadline until Christmas. Even so, it was a hard job to complete the 641 pages of full score in time, with the now obligatory help of Imogen Holst, together with Rosamund Strode, a professional soprano and postgraduate student of Imogen's. This was by far the longest purely orchestral score Britten was ever to write. *The Prince of the Pagodas* has a simple fairytale plot. The princess Belle Rose is spurned by her father, the Emperor of the Middle Kingdom, in favour of her wicked sister Belle Épine. She is carried off to Pagoda Land, where she meets a giant salamander, who reveals himself as a prince. The two of them return to the Middle Kingdom and free the Emperor from the clutches of Belle Épine, who has become Empress, before returning to idyllic happiness in Pagoda Land.

Even if *The Prince of the Pagodas* did not engage Britten on the same intensely personal level as, for example, the Violin Concerto or the *Serenade* or his operas, in many other respects it is one of his most important works. The sheer inventiveness of it is extraordinary – so many memorable ideas – as is the sustained brilliance of the orchestral writing. The quality of the music is the equal of the Tchaikovsky ballets, which served as Britten's model for a large part of the score (Duncan recalls that Britten told him he kept a score of *Sleeping Beauty* beside his bed while writing the piece).[173] Most fascinating of all, unsurprisingly, is the Balinese-influenced music for Pagoda Land. Britten creates his own gamelan from the struck instruments of the symphony orchestra, including gong, xylophone, vibraphone, harp, celesta and piano duet. The result is an astonishingly accurate replication of the original. This first extended use of gamelan-inspired music was to have huge implications for Britten's future work.

The Prince of the Pagodas was finally produced at Covent Garden on New Year's Day, 1957, and had a further 22 performances that year. It was a moderate success, but after 1960 was never produced again in Britten's lifetime, and since Britten fell out with Cranko over the latter's production of *A Midsummer Night's Dream*, he tended to forget about his ballet, as he had done with other pieces that summoned up unhappy memories.

During 1957 he and Pears decided they must move house. Life at 4 Crabbe Street had become difficult, now that Britten was so famous. As his sister Beth wrote: 'Passers-by would peer over the fence and, when they made the fence high, peered through the holes. There was no privacy.'[174] A practical solution presented itself: Mary Potter lived in the Red House, a substantial brick farmhouse half a mile from the town centre, on the edge of the golf course where Britten's father had often played. After her marriage ended, Mary Potter wanted somewhere smaller, so she suggested an exchange of houses with Britten and Pears. In December, while working on *Noye's Fludde*, Britten wrote to Edith Sitwell: *You can imagine the final bars of the opera are punctuated by hammer-blows! However we are now about half in, & can already see*

Britten leaving the Red House in his Alvis

that it is going to be lovely. A little further from the sea, but with a splendid garden, & it is a beautiful old house.[175] There was also a tennis court and a croquet lawn, and later a swimming pool was built, and a library. One of the outhouses was converted into a first-floor studio where, as Britten later told Edith Sitwell, he could *bang away to my heart's content.*[176] But in some ways the move was a sad one, for as Beth said: 'Ben could no longer work looking out at his beloved sea.'[177]

The first piece Britten wrote at the Red House was *Songs from the Chinese*, settings of Arthur Waley's translations for Pears and a new accompanist, the guitarist Julian Bream. He then immediately turned to *Noye's Fludde*, a theatre piece for children, his finest work in a genre he had more or less invented himself. The text was taken from the Chester Miracle Plays, whose direct, unsentimental language was an immediate safeguard against either the pious or the twee. As in *Saint Nicolas*, Britten cleverly combined amateur and professional instrumentalists and singers. He also again built congregational hymns into the structure of the piece. The opera begins with 'Lord Jesus, think on me', a confession of universal sin, and ends with Tallis's 'The spacious firmament on high', sung in canon to provide a resplendent conclusion. At its centre, the Victorian seafarers' hymn 'Eternal Father, strong to save' appears as the climax of the storm that initiates the flood – a passacaglia, whose theme happens to provide a perfect bass to the hymn. Aside from Noye, the intransigent Mrs Noye and the (spoken) Voice of God, all the parts are performed by children, who also play the majority of the instruments, including a multiplicity of recorders, eight bugles, 12 handbells and a range of unpitched percussion. The score is full of marvellous sounds evoking a vivid and happy childhood world: the recorder choir and open string pizzicatos for the building of the ark; the joyful shouts of 'Kyrie eleison' together with bugle chords (here purged of their military associations) for the procession of animals into the ark; the combination of piano and the specially invented 'slung mugs' for the first spots of rain; a fluttertonguing treble recorder for the dove who is sent out to find land; the gently dissonant sound of handbell clusters at the end, a kind of Christian gamelan, full of innocently sensual pleasure. Despite the authoritarian presence of the Voice of God, whose whims have caused all this mayhem, *Noye's Fludde* is largely a work free from guilt, a vision of earthly delights.

Life at the Red House eventually settled down into a routine, with the housekeeper Miss Hudson supervising the cooking as she had at 4 Crabbe Street. Britten liked plain food, the kind he had had at school, including rice pudding and 'spotted dog' (a suet pudding with sultanas). He had an intense dislike of shellfish, and of a number of other foods including mushrooms, tomatoes and pears. He liked most of all what Nellie Hudson called 'nursery food',[178] and would sometimes consume a whole tin of condensed milk. But he also had a taste for fine wines. Pears was more of a gourmet, and when he was there the cooking would be more elaborate. When composing, Britten kept to an orderly schedule. He rose early, took a cold bath (another legacy from his schooldays) and was at his desk from 9 till 1. In the afternoon he wrote letters and took a walk, in later years with his dachshunds, always paying keen attention to the birds he saw. While on his walk he also planned his next day's work. Tea was an important ritual. Significantly perhaps, Britten could not cook – according to Pears he could just about boil an egg – but he was adept at making tea, blending different varieties. Following tea, he returned to his studio until dinner at 8, after which there

Elizabeth (Nellie) Hudson (1898–1982) was Britten's housekeeper for 21 years from 1952. After her retirement in 1973 on her 75th birthday, she lived in Cosy Nook, a cottage built for her in the grounds of the Red House, which she had named herself. Cosy Nook is now administered by the Britten-Pears Foundation, and much of this book was written there.

might be a little reading, or listening to music on records, before early bed, often with the score of a string quartet.

At the 1958 Festival *Noye's Fludde* was premiered in Orford

Britten to Roger Duncan, 11 March 1957.
There's one thing I'd like you to do for me – if you haven't done it already – see if you can do the following addition sum, & see how long it takes you to do it

> CROSS
> ROADS *– you are told that the value of S is 3,*
> ———
> DANGER

& I guess that each letter stands for a different numeral.

Church. It was produced by Colin Graham, who became associated with almost all Britten's later operas. That year Britten wrote two new and especially fine song-cycles for Pears, some settings of Hölderlin with piano for the 50th birthday of Prince Ludwig of Hesse, and the *Nocturne* for tenor, seven obbligato instruments and strings. The two central poems of *Sechs Hölderlin-Fragmente*, 'Sokrates und Alcibiades' and 'Die Jugend', express Britten's own philosophy of beauty in ecstatic progressions of triads that recall the redemptive 'interview' music of *Billy Budd*. The *Nocturne* had its origin in a setting of Tennyson's 'Now sleeps the crimson petal' which Britten had originally written for the *Serenade*. He eventually found no place for it there, and was perhaps also wary of its openly erotic nature. Although the song does not appear in the *Nocturne*, its repeated rocking accompaniment figure for strings pervades the later cycle's opening song, Shelley's 'On a poet's lips I slept', and then acts as a ritornello linking the remaining seven songs. As in the *Serenade*, Britten chose a sequence of poems, here by eight different poets, all again on the same nocturnal theme, but darker and stranger than in the earlier work. The dark heart of the *Nocturne* is reached in two consecutive songs that look forward to the *War Requiem*: lines from Wordsworth's *Prelude* about fears of the French Revolution are set to a disquieting timpani accompaniment, anticipating the shell-fire drumbeats in Wilfred Owen's 'Be slowly lifted up' in the later work; this song is followed by

Britten's first setting of Owen, 'The Kind Ghosts', a chillingly seductive vision of death. Each of the songs has a different instrumentation, using the obbligato instruments in turn; the last, a Shakespeare sonnet, is a passionate love song, richly scored for the whole ensemble. As in the *Serenade* this last song brings benediction: the poet is happy because in sleep he dreams of his absent beloved. Here we seem to stand on the threshold of *A Midsummer Night's Dream*, to which Britten would soon turn.

First he had to get two commissions out of the way. One is a small masterpiece: the *Missa Brevis* for boys' voices and organ, written for George Malcolm, the organist of Westminster Cathedral, the Roman Catholic cathedral in London, and its choir. The sound of these strong-toned boys' voices was quite different from the softer, rounder tone of Anglican cathedral choirs. Britten was excited by this sound, and was further to exploit it in his *War Requiem*. The other commission is an outstanding piece of occasional music, if nothing more: the *Cantata Academica* for soloists, chorus and orchestra, composed for the 500th anniversary of the

While in New York in 1959, Pears made a last visit to Auden. He wrote to Britten on 12 February: 'Last night my dear Elizabeth [Mayer] & I went round to see Wystan & Chester at Lincoln's house [Lincoln Kirstein, for whose American Ballet Company Britten had written his Rossini suite *Matinées musicales* in 1941] – just round the corner. It was a very odd evening, with me inevitably being goaded into silly defiance & behaving odiously. Wystan looking like Oscar Wilde painted by Picasso or somebody was just the same as always, dogmatic[,] laying down the law about opera translators & librettos, Chester puffy & gossipy & Lincoln nervous & sensitive & dotty, with a nice wife. I got furious & the whole affair was hateful to me. I can't bear to see them again, tho' Chester threatens to ring & arrange a gossip! You would have adored it!' Britten replied (17 February): *Your picture of N. York was alarmingly clear – especially the ghastly evening with Wystan etc. – what is one to do about him? Nothing, I suppose – just keep away.*

University of Basle. Both here and in the *Cantata Misericordium* which he wrote four years later, Britten had to set rather ungainly Latin texts, and in a few places in the *Cantata Academica* at least, which he referred to in a letter to Plomer as his *Basel chore*, duty gets the better of inspiration.

Now he began the major task of a new opera. The Aldeburgh Festival was expanding under its energetic manager Stephen Reiss, who had taken over from Elizabeth Sweeting in 1955. Britten was keen to build a new theatre, and a site was found, but in order to save money it was decided instead to enlarge the Jubilee Hall. For its reopening on 11 June 1960 Britten decided to make a three-act operatic version of Shakespeare's *A Midsummer Night's Dream*. He and Pears made their own adaptation of the play, cutting it to half its length and omitting Shakespeare's Act I entirely, so that the opera opens in the magic wood and remains there until the final scene in Theseus' palace. All the elements of Shakespeare's drama, however, are present. There are the three intertwining worlds, each given its own characteristic music. The world of the fairies is marvellously evoked, with the fairies sung by boys, Oberon by a counter-tenor (Alfred Deller, who had revived this voice, created the role), while Puck is a speaking part played by a boy acrobat, always accompanied by solo trumpet and drum. *I got the idea of doing Puck like this in Stockholm*, Britten wrote, *where I saw some Swedish child acrobats with extraordinary agility and powers of mimicry.*[179] The tangled quartet of lovers, soon to be more confused by Puck's mistakes with his love potion, sing with passionate urgency, giving the lie to those who claim that Britten cannot write love music, let alone heterosexual love music. The rustics, Shakespeare's 'rude mechanicals', have appropriately down-to-earth music, full of deliberate clichés, culminating in their presentation of the play, 'Pyramus and Thisbe', which they have been rehearsing throughout the opera. Britten enjoys himself hugely here with parodies of bad 19th-century opera, including a Donizettian mad scene. The fairies' orchestra is full of exotic sounds: celesta, harpsichord, vibraphone; while the magic wood itself is unforgettably introduced by muted strings playing continuous ascending and descending glissandi. Britten used the largest orchestral forces he could fit into the Jubilee Hall, but had to restrict himself to 12 strings: for the Royal Opera House production in 1961 (and the recording in 1966) the string numbers were expanded.

Within the magic world he had created Britten felt secure, and *A Midsummer Night's Dream* is the most benign of all his operas. Oberon is a strange, yet not a sinister figure, and his punishment of Tytania, making her fall in love with the first creature she sees after waking, does not result in any serious wrong: her love scene in Act II with the 'translated' Bottom, which might have been grotesque, results in perhaps the most sensuously beautiful music that Britten ever composed. The closing ensemble of Act III also has exquisite, unearthly beauty, after the Fairy King and Queen are reconciled, all has been resolved in the mortal world and the fairies appear to give their blessing. Britten had been trying all his life to capture the perfection of innocence: here he does so.

In Peace I Have Found My Image

In September 1960, Britten met Shostakovich for the first time, sharing a box with him at the Royal Festival Hall in London for the British premiere of the Russian composer's First Cello Concerto. The two composers had enormous respect for each other and met on several subsequent occasions, the last time in 1972 when Shostakovich stayed at the Red House with his wife and he was given the rare privilege of seeing a half-completed Britten score: the draft of *Death in Venice*. Britten dedicated *The Prodigal Son* to Shostakovich, and in 1970 conducted the first performance outside Russia of Shostakovich's 14th Symphony, which was dedicated to him.

The soloist in Shostakovich's Concerto was Mstislav Rostropovich. Britten was so excited by his playing that when they met the following day he offered to write him a sonata for the two of them to play at Aldeburgh, thus inaugurating the warmest and most productive friendship of Britten's later life. He began composing it after Christmas, and on 17 January 1961 he wrote to Pears: *As far as I can I've got the cello piece in order, at least I must stop fiddling with it & get on with something else. I played it to Imo who was quite impressed, &, as if an omen, as soon as I'd played it over, the telephone rang & there was 'Slava' from Paris, & I had a wild & dotty conversation in broken German (very broken) with him. But he is a dear, & his warmth & excitement came over in spite of the bad line & the crazy language.*[180] Rostropovich was overjoyed with the five-movement Sonata when he received it in February. Britten was to write five more cello pieces for Rostropovich: the *Cello Symphony*, three solo suites, and a very late piece, the *Tema 'Sacher'* for a set of variations by 11 other composers to celebrate the 70th birthday of the conductor and new

Rostropovich and Britten, Armenia, 1965

music commissioner Paul Sacher. In addition he wrote a Pushkin
song-cycle, *The Poet's Echo*, for him to play on the piano with his
wife, the soprano Galina Vishnevskaya, who also became a close
friend. The three solo suites, composed in 1964, 1967 and 1971,
are the most important solo cello music since Bach. Like Bach's
suites, they are mostly based on Classical dance movements, but all
three suites contain fugues, a form that Bach included in his solo
violin sonatas but not his cello suites. Britten solves the inherent
technical problems very cunningly. The Third Suite, perhaps the
most searching of the three, ends with a movement based on
Russian folk songs arranged by Tchaikovsky and the Orthodox
Hymn for the Departed (also used by Tchaikovsky in his Sixth
Symphony).

By the time Rostropovich and Britten gave the premiere of the
Sonata at the 1961 Aldeburgh Festival, Britten had begun to
compose his *War Requiem*. He had been asked in 1958 to write a
piece for the consecration of the new Coventry Cathedral, built on
the ruins of the old cathedral which had been almost entirely

destroyed by bombs in 1940. He decided on a large-scale work for soloists, chorus and orchestra in memory of those who died in both world wars. His innovative plan was to intersperse the movements of the Requiem Mass, sung by solo soprano and chorus (with a separate boys' chorus), with settings for tenor and baritone solo and chamber orchestra of poems by Wilfred Owen, the outstanding English poet of the First World War. It was an integral part of his scheme that the three soloists should represent the three nations which, as he told Vishnevskaya, had suffered most during the last war: Britain, Germany and Russia. So Pears and Dietrich Fischer-Dieskau were the tenor and baritone soloists at the premiere, and Vishnevskaya was to have been the soprano. But the Soviet authorities would not let her sing standing next to a German, and so at the first performance the British soprano Heather Harper replaced her. Vishnevskaya did, however, take part in the later recording.

Owen's poems provide a telling and sometimes bitter commentary on the Requiem texts: there is no trace of piety here. The cumulative effect of the text is an acute criticism of conventional Christian attitudes to war, which makes the *War Requiem* more 'modern' than any of Britten's previous religious works, and arguably the most important pacifist statement that any 20th-century composer was to make. The two texts are closely integrated: thus the liturgical last trump in the *Dies Irae*, 'Tuba mirum, spargens sonum' ('the wondrous trumpet, scattering its sound') is followed by Owen's 'Bugles sang, saddening the evening air', and the lines from the *Offertorium*: 'quam olim Abrahae promisisti, et semini eius' ('which you once promised to Abraham, and his seed'), by Owen's recasting of the story of Abraham and Isaac. Britten actually quotes from his own Canticle II when the voice of God offers Abraham a reprieve from sacrificing Isaac; but Owen continues: 'the old man would not so, but slew his son, – / And half the seed of Europe, one by one', and the last line is repeated over

Conducting the *War Requiem*, Royal Albert Hall, 1963

and over again by the two male soloists while the boys' chorus return impotently to the words of the liturgy. The profoundest marriage of the two texts comes in the *Agnus Dei*, which acts as a refrain to the tenor's infinitely sad song 'One ever hangs where shelled roads part', and to which Britten adds his own 'Dona nobis pacem'.

The opening *Requiem Aeternam* begins in the tragic world of D minor familiar from the *Sinfonia da Requiem*. At the end of the work, after the apocalyptic climax of the *Libera Me*, comes Owen's 'Strange Meeting', about an English and a German soldier who encounter one another in the underworld of death: 'I am the enemy you killed, my friend.' The poem's last line, 'Let us sleep now', is mingled with the 'In paradisum' from the Requiem and the words are taken up by all the soloists and chorus in a great wave of benediction; it recalls the end of the *Sinfonia da Requiem* and its similar ebbing away into the sea that symbolizes both reconciliation and death.

With the *War Requiem* Britten reached the apex of his reputation: it was almost universally acclaimed as a masterpiece. The recording that Britten conducted seven months after the first performance on 30 May 1962 sold over 200,000 copies in the first year of its release. Almost no serious composer since has been able to communicate on such a wide scale, and on such an important theme. Owen wrote: 'All a poet can do is warn', and although the existence of the *War Requiem* has plainly done nothing to end war in our troubled world, Britten was right to make his own great warning statement.

Britten hoped to finish his next major piece, the Symphony for Cello and Orchestra, in time for him to conduct it with Rostropovich at a festival of British music in Moscow in March 1963, but during the winter of 1962–3 he was plagued once again by health problems, and so just missed his deadline. He returned to Moscow in March 1964 to conduct it with the Moscow Philharmonic Orchestra. Shostakovich and Khatchaturian were in the audience, and the Symphony was received so enthusiastically that the finale was encored. The Cello Symphony is once again cast in Britten's tragic key of D minor (did Britten originally associate D minor with tragedy because of Beethoven's Ninth Symphony, or could it have been Mahler's Ninth?). The first movement is one of his darkest, the music struggling upwards from the murky opening sounds of tuba, contrabassoon and basses, but continually being beaten down by timpani strokes. There is an 'all passion spent' coda and a final whispered cadence into D major, anticipating happier events to come. The scherzo is a swift, uncanny piece, somewhat akin to the Second Quartet's, but more disembodied. The timpani strokes return to punctuate the noble, tragic theme of the Adagio, whose middle section quietly introduces the tune of the finale, launched jubilantly in D major by a solo trumpet. (In the recording made of the first performance this tune is played in such a wonderfully abandoned manner by the Moscow trumpeter that one wonders if Britten had this particular sound in his head from the start.) The finale is cast in the familiar passacaglia form, but here in celebratory mood, ending with a coda whose lush thirds recall the Sibelius of the Fifth Symphony, and there is a similar feeling of achieved, secure – even ecstatic – happiness.

Much of 1963 was taken up with concerts celebrating Britten's 50th birthday, culminating in a concert performance of *Gloriana* at the Royal Festival Hall on the actual day, 22 November. Britten was nonetheless able to write two substantial works during the year: the *Cantata Misericordium*, a setting of the parable of the Good Samaritan for baritone, chorus and small orchestra for the centenary of the International Red Cross; and a *Nocturnal* for solo guitar for Julian Bream, based on Dowland's song 'Come, heavy sleep' – another night piece full of disturbing visions, but ending in recovered calm. Now he at last turned to a project he had been thinking about for eight years. In 1955, before going off on his Far East tour, he asked William Plomer what to see in Japan, and Plomer suggested the Noh theatre. It so chanced that the Noh play Britten saw in Tokyo in February 1956, *Sumidagawa*, was about an innocent boy who escapes from robbers holding him, but dies of exhaustion after crossing a river in a ferry boat; his mad mother comes to look for him, and the ferryman takes her to her son's grave. Britten, who had not expected to enjoy the performance, was much moved, and after he returned

With Clytie, 1960s

he talked to Plomer about turning *Sumidagawa* into an opera. The idea hung fire for some time, but by the end of 1958 Plomer had drafted a libretto, to which Britten responded enthusiastically. Then in April 1959 he wrote to Plomer about *the idea of making it a <u>Christian</u> work (Here you can stop reading & have another sip of coffee to give you courage to proceed) . . . I <u>can't</u> write Japanesy music . . . But we might get a very strong atmosphere (which I personally love) if we set it in pre-conquest East Anglia (where there were shrines galore).*[181] Plomer did not demur, and produced a new,

Christianized libretto, which Britten finally began setting in January 1964, during a visit to Venice. He wrote to John Piper: *Peter & I are settled in a rambling flat in a crazy old Palazzo on the Grand Canal. Very quiet & good for working in (only I'm a bit stupid so far). The weather is icy, & they all say (they always do) they've never known so much fog.*[182] It was here that *Curlew River*, as the new piece was called, was composed.

In transforming *Sumidagawa* into a Christian parable, Plomer and Britten gave the ending a miraculous aspect absent from the Buddhist stoicism of the original, where the mother weeps inconsolably for her son. In *Curlew River* the Madwoman, as Plomer called her (she is sung by a tenor, preserving the all-male Noh tradition) is rewarded for her constant hope: she hears her son singing from his grave; then his spirit appears and blesses her, and she becomes sane again. The rest of the story is close to the original, and although it is now a mystery play acted out by monks, who process in to their performing area to the plainsong hymn 'Te lucis ante terminum', which provides much of the musical material, the music retains an austere, non-Western quality. There is no conductor; the melodic lines are mostly unmeasured, and the players take their cues from one another. It is completely different from any music Britten had composed before. In spite of his disclaimer about 'Japanesy' music, there is a strong influence of Gagaku, both in the frequent use of heterophony and in the sound of the ensemble (there is much use of flute and drums and organ clusters that sound like the *sho*, a kind of Japanese mouth organ which Britten bought in Tokyo and taught himself to play). To the three instruments mentioned Britten adds only horn, viola and harp, plus the bell sounds – a single deep bell, then a range of high bells – that herald the miracle and suddenly bring light into the sombre landscape. At the climax of the work, the boy's treble voice soars over the ensemble, with a piccolo representing his disembodied spirit.

Britten creates a real feeling of transcendence here from his small resources.

Curlew River was first performed during the 1964 Aldeburgh Festival in the Norman church at Orford, an apt setting. Britten was already planning a sequel, based on the biblical story of Shadrach, Meshach and Abednego, who are cast into a fiery furnace by King Nebuchadnezzar for refusing to worship his golden image, but saved by their faith. *The Burning Fiery Furnace* was premiered in Orford at the 1966 Festival and was followed two years later by *The Prodigal Son*, thus completing a triptych of 'parables for church performance', as Britten called these pieces, based on the three cardinal virtues: hope, faith and charity. In *The Burning Fiery Furnace* Britten drew on the experience of writing *Curlew River* and the techniques he employs are more elaborate. The piece is still designed to be performed without a conductor, but much of the music is fast and rhythmic, and its sound world is more brilliant and colourful than the first parable. Britten invents his own Babylonian music, drawing on the biblical 'flute, harp, sackbut' (he adds an alto trombone to the ensemble), together with invented percussion – anvil, multiple whip, Babylonian Drum. The instrumentalists process around the church to a superbly inventive Babylonian march, followed by the hymn to the pagan god Merodak, which is full of barbaric splendour. The vocal writing for the three Israelites, who always sing together, is particularly skilful, and Britten remembered it when in 1971 he wrote what sounds like a companion piece, his Canticle IV, based on Eliot's poem 'Journey of the Magi'. The Canticle has its own moment of transcendence based on plainsong, when the melody 'Magi videntes stellam' is introduced to accompany the repeated word 'satisfactory': a quietly mysterious moment.

The third church parable, *The Prodigal Son*, was inspired by the Rembrandt painting that Britten had seen in the Hermitage Museum on a Christmas visit to Russia with Pears in 1966.

Despite some innovations in its musical language, for much of its length *The Prodigal Son* is a sad falling off from the high standard of the other two. The deadly hand of piety falls across the score. The most lively music occurs when the Tempter (the part originally sung by Pears), with his sprightly accompanying trumpet, lures the Younger Son away from his dull family towards the delights of the city. Yet the seductions of wine, women and gambling to which the Tempter introduces the Younger Son turn out to be as dreary as Britten's memories of the Paris brothel he visited before his mother's death. They are particularly unseductive because the boy tempters – a necessary condition of the all-male cast – are poor substitutes for women's voices. The quality of the music does, however, recover during the Younger Son's exhausted journey home, and his reduction to utter despair in desolate solo viola music that recalls the teenage *Elegy*.

In 1964 Britten changed his publisher. Since the deaths of Ralph Hawkes in 1950 and Erwin Stein in 1958, Britten had felt bereft of real support from Boosey & Hawkes. Donald Mitchell, who had been working on his behalf part-time at Booseys and was also adviser on music books to Faber & Faber, was able to persuade Faber's chairman Richard de la Mare to start a new, associated publishing company, Faber Music, expressly to publish Britten's music. Under Mitchell's directorship, Faber Music also took on other living composers and soon became one of the leading contemporary music publishers. Mitchell was the ideal supportive figure Britten needed, as his self-confidence was still precarious, liable to evaporate at the slightest provocation. Ronald Duncan tells a characteristic story of Britten during the provincial tour of *Lucretia* in 1946, walking painfully down a hotel corridor trying to avoid stepping on the red lines on the carpet. *If I can get right up and down the corridor without touching the lines*, Britten told him solemnly, *it will mean that I am a composer.*[183] Little had changed 18 years later: in November 1964 he was writing to Pears: *I've been*

From Britten's speech on receiving the First Aspen Award, 1964:

I certainly write music for human beings – directly and deliberately. I consider their voices, the range, the power, the subtlety, and the colour potentialities of them. I consider the instruments they play – their most expressive and suitable individual sonorities . . . I also take note of the human circumstances of music, of its environment and conventions; for instance, I try to write dramatically effective music for the theatre – I certainly don't think opera is better for not being effective on the stage (some people think that effectiveness must be superficial). And then the best music to listen to in a great Gothic church is the polyphony which was written for it, and was calculated for its resonance . . . I believe, you see, in occasional music . . . almost every piece I have ever written has been composed with a certain occasion in mind, and usually for definite performers, and certainly always human ones . . . I can find nothing wrong . . . with offering to my fellow-men music which may inspire them or comfort them, which may touch them or entertain them, even educate them – directly and with intention. On the contrary, it is the composer's duty, as a member of society, to speak to or for his fellow human beings.

madly low & depressed . . . worried about my work which seems so bad always . . . I <u>must</u> get a better composer somehow – but how – – but how – – –?[184] Meanwhile honours flooded in: 11 honorary doctorates, the First Aspen Award for 'the individual anywhere in the world judged to have made the greatest contribution to the advancement of the humanities', and in 1965 Britten was admitted to the Order of Merit, the highest award the Queen could confer. *Honours, as you know only too well, don't really touch one*, he wrote to Yehudi Menuhin, *but there are moments in one's depressions, when one feels one's work to be hopelessly inadequate (all too often!) that they <u>do</u> encourage.*'[185]

On his doctor's advice, Britten decided to make 1965 a sabbatical year from recitals and conducting. He and Pears took several long holidays. In January they went to India, where Britten was able to indulge his passion for bird-watching. He wrote to Rosamund Strode, who had succeeded Imogen Holst as his full-time music assistant, about their stay in Udaipur, north of Bombay: *we used to take trips around in a boat seeing the most fantas-*

tic birds – Pelicans, Storks & Cranes of all kinds, Ibis's, Cormorants & Darters, Stilts, Parrots etc. etc. – & crocodiles sunning themselves & eyeing us greedily![186] Britten was not taking a holiday from composing: during the Indian trip he wrote his *Gemini Variations* for the 13-year-old Hungarian Jeney twins. This light-hearted 'quartet for two players', based on a theme of Kodály, exploited the twins' ability to perform on flute, violin and piano duet. He also read *Anna Karenina* and made serious plans for an opera based on Tolstoy's novel, with Vishnevskaya in the leading role. Colin Graham, who since *Curlew River* had become his regular producer, drafted a libretto, but the plan came to grief after the Soviet invasion of Czechoslovakia in 1968, when it became impossible for Britten to accept a commission from the Bolshoi. This, and an earlier idea to write a *King Lear* for Fischer-Dieskau, are the chief casualties among Britten's various aborted opera projects.

Both Fischer-Dieskau and Vishnevskaya were at least given their own song-cycles with piano. Britten wrote *Songs and Proverbs of William Blake* for Fischer-Dieskau on his return from India in March. It is a sombre, deeply serious work, more concerned with experience than with innocence, and showing how strongly Britten responded to the subversive side of Blake. *The Poet's Echo*, settings of Pushkin in Russian, was written for Vishnevskaya while Britten and Pears were on their second long holiday, with the Rostropoviches, at a composers' colony in Armenia in August. The echoes described in the first song are hauntingly evoked in heterophonic canons, and the opening rising seventh becomes the insistently ticking clock of the final song, 'Lines written during a sleepless night'. When Britten and Pears gave an impromptu performance of the songs to Vishnevskaya, Rostropovich and the curators of the Pushkin birthplace museum at Mikhailovskoye, near Pskov, the clock outside struck midnight just as Britten was playing this final song. After it had finished all of them sat in spellbound silence.[187]

Back in Aldeburgh in October, Britten began writing *The Burning Fiery Furnace*, but he was not well again and made slow progress. He managed to finish the composition sketch by February 1966, then went into hospital to have an operation for diverticulitis, a disease of the colon. While convalescing he wrote a letter to Pears which shows their relationship still to be the central point of his life. His only other composition that year was *The Golden Vanity*, a 'Vaudeville' for boys' voices and piano, written for the Vienna Boys' Choir, a setting of a traditional ballad about a brave cabin boy who sinks a pirate ship and, having been promised a large reward, is left to drown by his heartless captain. Copland had set the same story for voice and piano in 1952, and Britten probably knew his version. Copland's piece is more matter-of-fact; Britten exploits the pathos of this story of another doomed innocent.

Britten to Pears, 3 April 1966:
I am sorry I have been such a drag on you these last years . . . It may not seem like it to you, but what you think or feel is really the most important thing in my life. It is an unbelievable thing to be spending my life with you; I can't think what the Gods were doing to allow it to happen! You have been so wonderful to me, given so much of your life, such wonderful experiences, knowledge and wisdom which I never could have approached without you. And above all – your love, which I never have felt so strongly as in the lowest moments, physically & spiritually, of that old op.

What's all this gush in aid of – only, really to say sorry for having mucked up your Easter plans, & to make quite sure that you realise that I love you!

B

Meanwhile, a major expansion of the Festival was in hand. Britten had long wanted to have a larger performing space. He had known the Maltings at Snape since he had lived in the Old Mill, and when in 1965 they were closed and buildings came up for rent, it was decided to turn one of them into a concert hall. Derek Sugden from the firm of Arup Associates – involved at the time with both the Sydney Opera House and the Queen Elizabeth Hall in London – was made responsible for the conversion, which was completed just in time for the opening of the 1967 Festival. On 2 June the Queen and Prince Philip came to lunch at the Red House and afterwards the Queen ceremonially opened the Maltings with a gold-plated key. Britten conducted the choir and the English Chamber Orchestra in his new version of the National Anthem (which began with a breathtaking *pianissimo*: it seems strange that no one had ever thought of this before, since the first verse is a prayer), a

Rehearsing with Pears, 1967

specially written overture, *The Building of the House*, and Delius's *Summer Night on the River*. Imogen Holst then conducted her father's *St Paul's Suite*, and Britten finished the concert with Handel's *Ode for St Cecilia's Day*. The acoustics of the hall turned out to be perfect, the best of any concert hall in Britain. The Festival, which had been gradually getting longer, was this year extended from two to three weeks. The Jubilee Hall was not made redundant – the premiere of Walton's Chekhov opera *The Bear* was given there – but the nature of the Festival inevitably changed with its being centred on the Maltings, and its old intimacy was lost, which some regretted.

After a lengthy recital tour with Pears in the autumn, which began in New York and went on to Mexico, through South America and right down to Chile, Britten was ready to start *The Prodigal Son*. He decided to rent the Palazzo Mocenigo in Venice again, where he had composed *Curlew River*. He wrote to Plomer on his return at the end of February: *To be in a place where man can still dominate (even over the pigeons!) somehow gives one confidence again in one's own capacity – machinery just has to take a back seat. I worked as almost never before, with the result that I'm about 3/4 done, & have a pretty clear idea of what's to follow.*[190] But there was soon a setback. In March he was taken ill with what he first thought was 'flu but, when his symptoms became more serious and he had to go into a hospital in Ipswich, was diagnosed as endocarditis, a consequence of his impaired heart. In spite of this he managed to finish *The Prodigal Son* in time for the 1968 Festival. He wrote another commissioned piece in the autumn, *The Children's Crusade*, a setting of a grim ballad by Brecht for children's voices and percussion, for the 50th anniversary of the Save the Children Fund, for which he supplied an appropriately dark-hued and at times quite violent score. The percussion that usually evoked images of liberation for him is used here to express an oppressive militarism.

He followed this piece with what was to be his last song-cycle for Pears and himself, *Who are these Children?*, to words by the Scottish poet William Soutar, who had died during the Second World War. Several of the poems allude to the war: one in particular, 'The Children', describes children killed by an air-raid and is full of the sound of sirens. The last song, 'The Auld Aik', about the felling of an oak tree, is monumentally simple and sad.

In 1967 the BBC commissioned Britten to write a full-length opera for television, and much of 1969 and 1970 was taken up with writing it. He had wanted to set another Henry James ghost story, *Owen Wingrave*, since he read it at the time of *The Turn of the Screw*. He approached Myfanwy Piper again to write the libretto. Owen Wingrave is a young man, the last scion of a military family, whose pacifist convictions compel him to reject the army career his family had planned for him. His parents are dead and he has been brought up by his aunt and a terrifying grandfather,

Sir Philip, a retired general. The latter, horrified when Owen tells them his decision, disinherits him; he is also rejected by his unyielding fiancée, Kate. She dares him to spend a night in a room in the family house haunted by the ghost of an ancestor who once killed his own young son in a fit of rage. Owen accepts, and is found dead the following morning. The arbitrary tragedy of his death, however, is subsidiary to the real point of the opera, which is Owen finding his true self and asserting his independence from the particular kind of repressive convention his family represents. In his climactic 'peace' aria in Act II he proclaims: 'In peace I have found my image, / I have found myself'. 'Peace' here does not stand simply for pacifism but for all the values Britten stood for, including the rightness of his own sexual choices. The music moves through a series of quiet triads, once again recalling the 'interview' music in *Billy Budd*; over these triads the percussion float a gamelan music that symbolizes freedom and ideal beauty. Then, in a chillingly expressionistic passage, with brilliant use of *Sprechstimme*, Owen confronts the apparitions of the ancestor and his son and declares his victory over them. Kate appears and

their anguished duet ends up with her accusing Owen of cowardice; in reply, he enters the haunted room, to an exultant C major chord with added sixth over a bass G: a similar chord to those at the end of Schoenberg's *Gurrelieder* and

Outside the Maltings, 1967

Mahler's *Das Lied von der Erde* – two ecstatic gestures of acceptance. It is one of the great moments in Britten's music.

Britten had hardly started on *Owen Wingrave* when he had to overcome a wholly unexpected trauma: the Maltings burned down as a result of an accidental fire on the first night of the 1969 Festival. The Festival continued nonetheless: only one event had to be cancelled, and the planned production of Mozart's *Idomeneo* was transferred to Blythburgh Church. Britten was determined that the Maltings would be rebuilt by next year's Festival, which it was. But the strain of these unexpected problems cannot have helped his increasingly precarious health. In February 1970 he and Pears bought a house just outside the village of Horham, 25 miles from Aldeburgh in deepest Suffolk. He had for some while been troubled at the Red House by the sound of low-flying aircraft from the nearby American base at Bentwaters. Chapel House, Horham would now become his composing retreat, and he had a small studio built – similar to Mahler's composing huts – at the bottom of the garden.

In March and April Britten and Pears visited Australia, where the EOG were performing the three church parables at the Adelaide Festival. After Adelaide Britten went with the painter Sidney Nolan and his wife Cynthia into the desert, which greatly impressed him: *it is pretty forbidding, but the light & the heat & sand do wonderful things – the most vivid colours, strangest shapes, oddest effects,*[189] he wrote to the teenage pianist Ronan Magill, with whom he had recently formed a close friendship. Britten and Nolan talked of collaborating on a ballet on an Aboriginal theme, which sadly came to nothing.

After *Owen Wingrave* was finally completed in August 1970, he began to make plans for his next, and as it turned out, his last opera. It would be for Peter – the longest and most demanding role Britten was ever to write for him – and on a story that summed up many of his lifelong preoccupations: *Death in Venice.*

Death Will Give Me Freedom

Thomas Mann's novella *Death in Venice* is one of his supreme artistic achievements. A middle-aged novelist, Gustav von Aschenbach, travels to Venice to try to recover the inspiration he has lost. At his hotel he sees a beautiful young Polish boy, Tadzio, and becomes infatuated with him. Despite warnings of a plague of cholera in Venice, Aschenbach stays on in pursuit of the boy, whom he admits to himself he loves, but with whom he never exchanges a word. He becomes ill with the cholera and dies. Mann weaves a web of extended meaning around this simple story.

Aschenbach, as an artist, is a devotee of Apollo, pursuing an ideal

Britten in his garden studio with Gilda

of Classical beauty and order in contrast to Romantic abandon, but in his rejection of disorder he risks becoming the sterile bourgeois artist of Auden's 1942 letter. In Venice, the city dedicated to beauty and sensual pleasure, Aschenbach encounters a personification of the beautiful, whom he approaches at first in a spirit of Apollonian purity. When he falls in love with the boy, he begins to feel the Dionysian ecstasy as well; but Dionysus is a dangerous god, and Aschenbach's encounter brings about his own destruction. Britten confronts this dilemma directly: it was a familiar part of his own life. In his frequent attachments to adolescent boys, his muse figures, he was continually reliving the story of *Death in Venice*, and the city itself had also become special to him. Britten spells out the morality of his and Aschenbach's situation with terrible honesty. Aschenbach asks himself at the end of the opera, as he muses on Plato's *Phaedrus*:

> Does beauty lead to wisdom, Phaedrus?
> Yes, but through the senses . . .
>
> And senses lead to passion, Phaedrus
> And passion leads to the abyss.

And so, it seems, Aschenbach has to die. He dies as he watches Tadzio walk into the sea: a fitting and, in some ways, a beautiful death. But is it all?

It is not all, as Britten's music tells us. For immediately after the 'Phaedrus aria' comes a warm, passionate outburst on the full orchestra in which, as in the D minor interlude in Berg's *Wozzeck*, the composer, as it were, steps onto the stage to plead for his hero. The music is based on a motif associated with Aschenbach's view of the sea from his hotel window. The orchestral postlude after Aschenbach's death takes this redemptive process a stage further. Over a deep, tolling bass, the strings gently restate Aschenbach's

Hymn to Apollo, which he had sung exultantly at the end of Act I; the hymn rises yearningly upward towards Tadzio's theme which is suspended above it on the glockenspiel, the two themes reaching a high unison A in the very last bar. It is a precarious affirmation, but an affirmation nonetheless. And so, at the last moment, Plato has been proved wrong: beauty and love have led to redemption. The end of *Death in Venice* is close in spirit to the end of *Tristan*.

Myfanwy Piper made a skilful adaptation of Mann's novella. There are only two main singing roles: Aschenbach, written for Pears, and a part for a bass-baritone, originally sung by John Shirley-Quirk, for the various representations of Death whom Aschenbach encounters. The Voice of Apollo, who presides over the games at the end of Act I in which Tadzio is victorious, is given to a counter-tenor. A mixed chorus populates the hotel and the city. Tadzio, his mother and their family and friends are played by silent dancers. This imaginative idea (an innovative extension of the balletic tradition in opera) solved the inherent problem of giving Tadzio a voice, when we see him only through Aschenbach's eyes. Tadzio has, however, his own distinctive sound world: in contrast to Aschenbach's frequently dark and introspective music, based on a 12-note series (shades of Leverkühn in Mann's *Doktor Faustus!*), Tadzio's is the light, lively sound of tuned percussion, and is Britten's most sophisticated treatment of his gamelan style.

Britten uses the expanded chamber orchestra he had used for *Owen Wingrave*, but his writing is spare and transparent. Only in a few significant places is the full orchestra used: one is where Aschenbach dares to make his avowal 'I love you', another the 'view' transfiguration described above. The vocal writing bears all the fruit of Britten's long experience, and exploits the freedom from the barline he had discovered through the church parables. Every word can be heard; as always, the timing is impeccable. In this, his farewell to opera, Britten confirms his place together with Strauss, Janáček and Berg in that small group of 20th-century opera composers who have demonstrated total mastery of their theatrical craft.

The composition of *Death in Venice* occupied Britten from December 1971 to March 1973, the initial stage while he was staying at Schloss Wolfsgarten with Peg Hesse, who was now widowed. There were frequent interruptions: most prominently the Festival, at which he conducted *The Turn of the Screw*, and Schumann's *Scenes from Goethe's Faust* – which he also recorded two months later. In August 1972 it was discovered that his heart problem had become serious enough to necessitate major surgery. He decided to finish the opera first, despite the obvious risks. At the end of March 1973, after another visit to Wolfsgarten for Peg Hesse's 60th birthday, Britten went to London to see a specialist recommended by Ian Tait, his Aldeburgh doctor. In May he was admitted to the National Heart Hospital to have a valve replaced: a valve made from human tissue was decided on rather than a mechanical one. The operation took six hours and was not completely successful: he had a slight stroke, probably caused by a fragment of calcium getting into his bloodstream and thence to his brain. The coordination of his right hand was affected. Rita Thomson, the senior sister who had looked after him while he was in hospital, accompanied him home to Suffolk. He had much appreciated her care for him and the following year when she decided to leave the Heart Hospital, Ian Tait engaged her as a full-time nurse. Britten became devoted to her, the last of many mother figures in his life, and she to him.

He could not attend the first performances of *Death in Venice* at the 1973 Festival, but in September a special performance was arranged for him at the Maltings. Later that month came the deaths of William Plomer and then Auden. Donald Mitchell was with Britten when he heard the news of Auden's death:

Britten wept for his old friend, whom he had not seen since 1953.

In November his 60th birthday was extensively celebrated by the BBC. He was still very weak. He had hoped that he would recover completely, but this was not to be the case. The new valve did not substantially improve his still abnormally enlarged heart, nor did his right hand return to normal, so that, as he soon realized, he would never again be able to play the piano to his own satisfaction. He did play piano duets with an Aldeburgh friend, Pat Nicholson, but these sessions left him depressed and he eventually gave them up. He had started to work once more, however, at first on retouchings to *Death in Venice* and on a revised version of the String Quartet in D major he had written at the Royal College; then on a new piece, the fifth of his Canticles and another setting of Eliot, the early poem 'The Death of Saint Narcissus', which Britten wrote for Pears and the harpist Osian Ellis. It is a strange poem: *I haven't got the remotest idea what it's about*,[190] Britten told Rosamund Strode; but it had enticing lines: 'He could not live men's ways, but became a dancer before God . . . He danced on the hot sand / Until the arrows came.' Narcissus is another figure from his magic world of dreams and ideal beauty.

In October 1974 Britten began an orchestral work which he finished in mid-November, the *Suite on English Folksongs*, subtitled 'A time there was . . . ', a reference to the final song of *Winter Words*. It was dedicated 'lovingly and reverently' to the memory of Percy Grainger, whose folk song arrangements he had always admired above all others, and which had inspired his own many arrangements. One of the movements, 'Hankin Booby', a rough, boisterous piece for wind and brass, he had composed for the opening of the Queen Elizabeth Hall in London in 1967. He now added four more, ending with a long and infinitely sad meditation on Grainger's transcription of the folk song 'Lord Melbourne', played in Grainger's exact notation by the cor anglais. The movement reaches a disturbing climax, with a muted trumpet call reminiscent of Holst's *Egdon Heath*, before it dies away on the *Das Lied von der Erde* added sixth chord: it is the first of Britten's farewells. The next, a less acquiescent one, followed immediately. *Sacred and Profane*, his final work for unaccompanied voices, was composed in December for the Wilbye Consort, a madrigal group that Pears had founded. The texts are medieval English lyrics and the last song, 'A Death', is a grim catalogue of the ills of old age, to which Britten reacts first with horror, then with gallows humour. Both these pieces showed that he was still able to compose anew with all his old vitality. At the same time, he was also revising *Paul Bunyan*. Auden's death had made this possible; previously, Britten would have had to consult him. When he heard the radio broadcast of this new version of his long suppressed and almost forgotten opera in February 1976, he broke down, overwhelmed by the strength of the music and the youthful optimism which was now so remote from him.

In 1975 his renewed creativity reached its peak, and he wrote his two last masterpieces, the cantata *Phaedra* and the Third String Quartet. *Phaedra* was written for Janet Baker, who had sung Lucretia both on stage and in the recording of the opera

Britten's last letter to Pears was written in February 1975[191] when Pears had fallen ill while staying with his duo partner, the harpist Osian Ellis.

My darling, I am so sorry that your temp. is up again – but you must try to be very patient. Can you read? I am sure there'll be nice books around you. Or what about going on with that diary? – don't be shy of saying what happened in N.Y. at the Met!

It is lovely that you are with the Ellis' – how glad I am you aren't stuck in a hotel – St Enoch's! [When Pears was in Glasgow in 1972 he had spent a 'feverish and nightmarish' few days at St Enoch's Hotel.[192]]

I hope that by some miracle you can get here & we can look after you! In the meantime just

Love – love – love –

B.

Britten had conducted in 1970. *Phaedra* is a successor to *The Rape of Lucretia* and to *Death in Venice*: another story of fated love, whose end is death. It is highly operatic, and modelled on the Italian cantatas of Handel, using a harpsichord for the recitatives. The words are taken from Robert Lowell's free translation of Racine's play *Phèdre*, and describe Phaedra's 'thick adulterous passion' for her stepson Hippolytus, her guilt, and her decision to take poison: 'Death will give / me freedom; oh it's nothing not to live; / death to the unhappy's no catastrophe!' Britten sets these words with compelling intensity; they are followed by a grave meditation for the strings on the rising scale to which the last line is set. At the very end of the piece, after Phaedra has sung her last word, which

Hans Keller (1919–85) was born into a well-to-do and culturally well-connected family in Vienna: as a boy, his musical mentor was the same Oskar Adler who decades earlier had been Schoenberg's boyhood friend and first teacher. Forced to flee Austria after the 1938 *Anschluss*, Keller made a life in London – initially as a freelance violinist and viola-player, but soon finding his niche as a highly prolific and provocative writer on music as well as an influential teacher, lecturer and coach. An original thinker never afraid of controversy, Keller's passionate support of composers he saw as under-valued or insufficiently understood made him a tireless advocate of Britten and Schoenberg as well as an illuminating analyst of figures such as Mozart, Haydn, Beethoven and Mendelssohn. Much of his advocacy was carried out from within the BBC, where he came to hold several senior positions. Keller's gift for systematic thinking, allied to his philosophical and psychoanalytic knowledge, bore fruit in his method of 'Wordless Functional Analysis' (designed to furnish audible demonstrations of a masterwork's 'background unity') and a 'Theory of Music' which focuses on the 'meaningful contradiction of expectations'. He was married to the artist Milein Cosman, whose drawings illustrated some of his work, and who has drawn many musicians including Britten.

Britten in Venice, 1975

is 'purity', there is a moment of release, as the *Das Lied* added sixth chord again (with an additional D) is sounded over a sustained low C, and above it are heard fragments of Phaedra's song, which drift away as if blown by a breeze.

The Third Quartet was dedicated to Hans Keller, the Austrian emigré musician who had been writing with great insight and acute psychological penetration on Britten's music since the time of *Peter Grimes* and the Second String Quartet, of which he had published an analysis in 1947. Some time after this, Keller had a long conversation with Britten about string quartets and sonata form, at the end of which Britten said: *One day, I'll write a string quartet for you*.[193] And although the Third Quartet's five movements have titles, as if Britten was thinking in terms of a suite, the piece is in fact his last and finest tribute to Classical sonata form. The piece begins in near darkness, with a questing first movement in which the tonality is frequently obscured. A scherzo, full of vital energy, with a striding bass line, provides the bridge to a rapt slow movement, whose middle section is a cascade of bird songs that Britten heard while he was composing this movement in Horham; it ends in the purest C major, Britten's own special key. A disruptive second scherzo is called 'Burlesque', surely a reference to the 'Rondo Burlesque' in Mahler's Ninth Symphony, with which it shares an A minor tonality and a bitterly satirical mood. In the trio the viola plays figurations on the 'wrong side of [the] bridge': Britten was still inventing new sounds right at the end of his life. The finale is subtitled 'La Serenissima', and its introduction, which returns to the twilight world of the first movement, presents five quotations from *Death in Venice*, ending with the 'I love you' motif, on which the melody of the main movement, a passacaglia, is based.

From David Matthews's journal, 17 December 1975:

Colin & I went to Aldeburgh to play Ben's newly completed 3rd Quartet to him in piano duet. He has not changed too much in appearance; his voice is just a little less firm, but otherwise, when seated, he looks extremely well. But he mostly has to be helped to walk, and he can only work a few hours each day. We made rather a botched job of the piece playing it through by ourselves before lunch – at least I did; I was rather self-conscious at making so many mistakes & tended to get worse instead of improve. But after lunch . . . & a little more practice we did produce a reasonable through-performance for him, & it was a moving occasion as the quartet is certainly a masterpiece & proves his creative powers are quite undiminished. The long passacaglia finale is especially fine, a serene piece in E major. After we had finished there was a silence and then Ben said, in a small voice: *Do you think it's any good?* We assured him that it was.

How fitting that Britten's last great work should end with the last of his passacaglias. Britten wrote this movement on his final visit to Venice in November 1975; the passacaglia bass, with nice appropriateness, was derived from the sound of the bells of Santa

Maria della Salute, which are heard only once a year, on 21 November, when they commemorate Venice's salvation from a 17th-century plague. The finale grows in strength and radiance in Aschenbach's key of E major, and we cannot but feel that the redemptive process which had begun at the end of *Death in Venice* is continued here. The work does not end in E major, but with a profound question, an unresolved chord and a lingering final D in the cello. It is as if, having laid Aschenbach properly to rest, Britten was setting off into new territory, which he did not live to explore.

Britten's health deteriorated in his final year, 1976, but he kept on working. He made a version for string orchestra of his viola and piano *Lachrymae*, deepening and darkening the piece, and arranged a final set of folk songs for voice and harp. He was able to attend the performance of *Paul Bunyan* at the Aldeburgh Festival, but looked shockingly ill. During the Festival he accepted a peerage, choosing the title Baron Britten of Aldeburgh. He was the first composer to have been ennobled in this way. In July he went on holiday to Norway with Pears and Rita Thomson, and while there sketched out a *Welcome Ode* for young people's choir and orchestra, intended for a concert to celebrate the Queen's Silver Jubilee in Ipswich the following year. He also began *Praise We Great Men*, a choral and orchestral work based on a poem Edith Sitwell had written for him in 1959, for Rostropovich to conduct in Washington D C. Colin Matthews, who had been helping by playing his music through on the piano, orchestrated the *Welcome Ode* for him, and was to start work on *Praise We Great Men*, but by the beginning of November Britten realized he could no longer compose. Pears, who had been on tour in Canada, returned home. On his 63rd birthday, 22 November, Britten was in bed and weak enough to need oxygen, but Rita Thomson organized a champagne party and his invited friends, who included Imogen Holst, Mary Potter, Peg Hesse,

Ben and Peter, May 1976

and his sisters Barbara and Beth, came up to his room one by one to say a last goodbye. A few days later Rostropovich made his farewell visit, and Britten gave him what he had written of *Praise We Great Men*, about two-fifths of the piece.

In the early hours of 4 December the end came. Pears was alone with him during his last moments and Britten died peacefully in his arms. 'He was certainly not afraid of dying,' Pears said. 'There was no struggle to keep alive . . . his greatest feeling was sadness and sorrow at the thought of leaving . . . his friends and his responsibilities.'[194] At the funeral in the Parish Church, the choir sang the *Hymn to the Virgin* that he had written when he was 16. He was buried in Aldeburgh churchyard, a short distance from the sea. Pears stayed on at the Red House, and continued to sing Britten's music around the world until 1980, when he had a stroke – which did not end his career, as he was still occasionally able to take part in concerts as a reciter. He died in 1986, and was buried next to his partner. Nearby is the grave of Imogen Holst, who had died two years before. So in death, Britten is close to two of the people who had loved him most.

Notes

SOURCES: ABBREVIATED LIST

L: *Letters from a Life: The Selected Letters and Diaries of Benjamin Britten 1913–1976*, Volumes 1 and 2, ed Donald Mitchell and Philip Reed (Faber & Faber, London, 1991). The first two volumes of a projected multi-volume series cover the years 1923 to 1945 and are an essential guide to understanding Britten's life and personality as a youth and young man. Donald Mitchell's introduction and the copious footnotes provide massive additional insight.

D: Britten's diaries, 1928–1938, unpublished (though substantial extracts appear in Volume 1 of *Letters from a Life*) – The Britten-Pears Library, Aldeburgh. Britten wrote daily entries in pocket diaries from 1928 until November 1937, and they continue with some gaps until the last entry on 16 June 1938, after which he only recorded appointments. At the start the entries tend to be brief and impersonal, but the record of the last few years forms a rich and revealing autobiography.

HC: Humphrey Carpenter, *Benjamin Britten: a Biography* (Faber & Faber, London, 1992). This first comprehensive biography provides an uninhibitedly frank account of Britten's life and a personal response to his music. Carpenter's assiduous research and his many interviews with Britten's surviving friends and acquaintances give his book an impressive depth.

1 Elias Canetti, *Crowds and Power* (Victor Gollancz, London, 1962), p.172
2 Transcript of interview by Donald Mitchell with Peter Pears for *The Tenor Man's Story*, directed by Barrie Gavin, Central Television, 1985
3 Interview with Henry Comer, CBC, 11 April 1968
4 Beth Britten, *My Brother Benjamin* (Kensal Press, Bourne End, 1986), p.17
5 D, 15 May 1937
6 Letter from Britten to Eric Walter White, 2 December 1953
7 L, p.12
8 L, p.81
9 L, p.107
10 'Britten Looking Back', *Sunday Telegraph*, London, 17 November 1963, p.9
11 Ibid
12 L, p.101
13 D, 11 May 1933
14 D, 21 September 1928
15 D, 24 June 1929
16 Murray Schafer, *British Composers in Interview* (Faber & Faber, London, 1963), p.119
17 D, 1 February 1930
18 L, p.224

19 D, 13 March 1929

20 D, 20 November 1929

21 D, 7 April 1930

22 Information from Jennifer Doctor

23 HC, p.32

24 L, p.191

25 D, 27 July 1930

26 D, 31 July 1930

27 D, 1 August 1930

28 *High Fidelity Magazine*, December 1959

29 L, p.133

30 L, p.133

31 D, 22 October 1931

32 D, 26 February 1931

33 D, 3 December 1930

34 L, p.351

35 D, 20 September 1930

36 D, 6 May 1931

37 D, 4 February 1931

38 D, 31 July 1934

39 D, 28 January 1931

40 D, 27 January 1932

41 D, 9 January 1931

42 L, p.202

43 D, 23 September 1930

44 'On Behalf of Gustav Mahler', *Tempo*, 2/2, American Series, February 1942, p.5; reprinted in *Tempo*, 120, March 1977, p.14

45 D, 6 May 1931

46 D, 2 February 1936

47 Ralph Vaughan Williams, *National Music and Other Essays* (Oxford University Press, 1987), p.187

48 D, 23 March 1936

49 D, 22 July 1932

50 D, 25 February 1936

51 D, 8 February 1933

52 D, 13 February 1933

53 'Britten Looking Back'

54 L, p.391

55 D, 19 April 1936

56 D, 30 November 1936

57 D, 22 December 1932

58 L. p.297

59 L, p.319

60 D, 13 November 1934

61 D, 5 July 1935

62 D, 6 March 1937

63 D, 18 March 1936

64 Beth Britten, *My Brother Benjamin*, p.92

65 HC, p.88

66 D, 31 January 1937

67 Sigmund Freud, translated James Strachey, 'Three Essays on the Theory of Sexuality', in *The Penguin Freud Library*, vol 7 (Penguin Books, London, 1977), p.56

68 L, p.18

69 D, opening entry 1936

70 D, 3 February 1936

71 D, 22 April 1936

72 D, 12 January 1937

73 HC, pp.20–25

74 D, 15 April 1936

75 D, 11 April 1937

76 Christopher Isherwood, *Christopher and his Kind: 1929–1936* (Avon Books, New York, 1977), pp.267–8

77 Donald Mitchell, *Britten and Auden in the Thirties* (Faber & Faber, London, 1981), p.149

78 L, p.503

79 D, 28 July 1937

80 Aaron Copland and Vivian Perlis, *Copland: 1900 through 1942* (Faber & Faber, London, 1984), p.293

81 L, p.577

82 Letter from Auden to Britten, undated (August 1938)

83 L, pp.562–3

84 Letter from Lennox Berkeley to Britten, 24 December 1938

85 L, p.605

86 Interview with Donald Mitchell, 15 September 1989 – The Britten-Pears Library

87 Letter from Wulff Scherchen to Britten, 19 January 1939; Letter from Britten to Wulff Scherchen, 22 January 1939

88 L, p.603

89 L, p.618

90 Interview with Donald Mitchell, 15 September 1989

91   L, p.634

92   L, p.644

93   L, p.663

94   L, p.665

95   L, p.759

96   Letter from Britten to Wulff Scherchen, 9 June 1939

97   L, p.668

98   L, p.702

99   L, p.724

100 Mervyn Cooke, *Britten and the Far East* (The Boydell Press, Woodbridge, 1998), pp.23–49

101 L, p.714

102 Christopher Palmer, 'The Orchestral Song-Cycles', in Palmer, ed, *The Britten Companion* (Faber & Faber, London, 1984), p.312

103 L, p.715

104 HC, p.147

105 L, p.759

106 L, p.849

107 L, p.921

108 BBC radio broadcast, 11 August 1965

109 Interview with Donald Mitchell, 23 October 1992 – The Britten-Pears Library

110 Interview with Mark Doran, April 1988, subsequently broadcast on BBC Radio York

111 L, pp.1037–8

112 L, p.1037

113 L, p.1046

114 L, p.1151

115 Imogen Holst's Diary, 10 October 1952 – The Britten-Pears Library

116 Michael Tippett, *Those Twentieth Century Blues* (Hutchinson, London, 1991), p.117

117 Ibid, p.117

118 L, p.1083

119 L, p.1088

120 L, p.1144

121 L, p.1037

122 Philip Brett, ed, *Benjamin Britten, Peter Grimes* (Cambridge Opera Handbooks, 1983), p.105

123 L, p.1037

124 Philip Brett, ed, *Benjamin Britten: Peter Grimes*, p.149

125 Ibid, p.149

126 L, p.1128

127 L, p.1268

128 L, p.1089

129 HC, p.228

130 L, p.1285

131 Letter from Britten to Pears, 24 January 1946

132 *John Betjeman's Collected Poems* (John Murray, London, 1958), p.80

133 Letter from Britten to Imogen Holst, 22 August 1946

134 HC, p.239

135 Letter from Tippett to Britten, undated, but either 21 or 28 July 1946

136 Britten and others, *The Rape of Lucretia, a Symposium* (The Bodley Head, London, 1948), p.8

137 HC, p.242

138 HC, p.240

139 L, p.65

140 Letter from Britten to Pears, 17 March 1948

141 Eric Walter White, *Stravinsky: the Composer and his Works* (Faber & Faber, London, 1966), p.480

142 Eric Crozier, 'Notes on Benjamin Britten', unpublished – The Britten-Pears Library

143 Donald Mitchell and Hans Keller, ed, *Music Survey: 1949–1952* (Faber Music, London, 1981), vol II, p.237

144 Aldeburgh Festival Programme Book, 1949, p.30

145 HC, eg pp.319–21, 376–7, 520–29

146 Alan Blyth, *Remembering Britten* (Hutchinson, London, 1981), p.139

147 Letter from Forster to Britten, undated (early December 1950), quoted in P N Furbank, *E M Forster: A Life* (Harcourt Brace Jovanovich, New York and London), Vol II, p.285

148 Donald Mitchell and Hans Keller, eds, *Benjamin Britten: A Commentary on his Works from a Group of Specialists* (Rockliff, London, 1952)

149 Imogen Holst's diary, 5 February 1953

150 Letter from Britten to Marion Harewood, 4 March 1951

151 Letter from Britten to Crozier, 7 December 1951

152 Letter from Crozier to Britten, 8 December 1951

153 HC, p.305

154 George, Earl of Harewood, *The Tongs and the Bones: The Memoirs of Lord Harewood* (Weidenfeld and Nicolson, London, 1981), p.134

155 Eric Crozier, 'Notes on Benjamin Britten'

156 Britten to Plomer, 24 July 1952

157 Britten to Basil Coleman, 6 October 1952

158 Paul Banks, ed, *Britten's* Gloriana: *Essays and Sources* (The Boydell Press, Woodbridge, 1993), p.21

159 Ibid, p.13

160 Ibid, p.67

161 Letter from Britten to Plomer, undated (July 1953)

162 D, 1 June 1932

163 Henry James, *The Art of the Novel: Critical Prefaces*, ed Richard P Blackmur (Charles Scribner's Sons, New York, 1934), p.176

164 Patricia Howard, ed, *Benjamin Britten: The Turn of the Screw* (Cambridge Opera Handbooks, 1985), p.106

165 Letter from Britten to Myfanwy Piper, 3 January 1954

166 HC, p.358

167 Letter from Britten to Edith Sitwell, 28 April 1955

168 Letter from Britten to Edith Sitwell, 27 September 1954

169 Britten to Barbara Britten, 26 December 1954

170 Ronald Duncan, *Working with Britten: A Personal Memoir* (The Rebel Press, Welcombe, 1981), p.132

171 Letter from Britten to Roger Duncan, 11 March 1956

172 Letter from Britten to Imogen Holst, 17 January 1956

173 Duncan, *Working with Britten*, p.136

174 Beth Britten, *My Brother Benjamin*, p.192

175 Letter from Britten to Edith Sitwell, 14 December 1957

176 Letter from Britten to Edith Sitwell, 3 March 1959

177 Beth Britten, *My Brother Benjamin*, p.192

178 Blyth, *Remembering Britten*, p.97

179 Christopher Palmer, ed, *The Britten Companion*, p.179

180 Letter from Britten to Pears, 17 January 1961

181 Letter from Britten to Plomer, 15 April 1959

182 Letter from Britten to John Piper, 25 January 1964

183 Duncan, *Working with Britten*, p.86

184 Letter from Britten to Pears, 17 November 1964

185 Letter from Britten to Menuhin, 16 May 1965

186 Letter from Britten to Rosamund Strode, 29 January 1965

187 *The Travel Diaries of Peter Pears 1936–1978*, ed Philip Reed (The Boydell Press, Woodbridge, 1995), pp.132–3

188 Letter from Britten to Plomer, 20 February 1968

189 Letter from Britten to Ronan Magill, 1 April 1970

190 HC, p.565

191 This letter is undated

192 *The Travel Diaries of Peter Pears*, p.173

193 *Hans Keller: Essays on Music*, ed Christopher Wintle (Cambridge University Press, 1994), p.111

194 *A time there was...: A Profile of Benjamin Britten*, directed by Tony Palmer, London Weekend Television, 1980

Chronology

Year	Age	Life
1913		Born 22 November at Lowestoft.
1918	5	First piano lessons from his mother. First compositions.
1921	8	Piano lessons with Miss Ethel Astle, teacher at local pre-preparatory school.
1923	10	Enters South Lodge Preparatory School as a day boy. Begins viola lessons with Audrey Alston.
1924	11	Hears Frank Bridge's orchestral suite, *The Sea*, at Norwich Triennial Festival.
1925	12	Overture in B flat, for full orchestra.
1926	13	Passes Grade VIII Associated Board piano examination with honours.
1927	14	Meets Bridge, and begins composition lessons with him.
1927–8		Head Boy of South Lodge, captain of cricket and *Victor Ludorum*.
1928	15	Enters Gresham's School, Holt. Continues composition lessons with Bridge; piano lessons with Harold Samuel in London.
1929	16	*The Birds* (Belloc song).
1930	17	Leaves Gresham's. Wins open scholarship to Royal College of Music, London (begins September). Composition lessons with John Ireland. Piano lessons with Arthur Benjamin. *Hymn to the Virgin*.
1931	18	Wins Ernest Farrar Prize for composition. String Quartet in D major.
1932	19	Sinfonietta, Op 1; Phantasy Quartet, Op 2.
1932–3		Active association with Macnaghten-Lemare concerts of new music at Ballet Club Theatre.

Year	Age	Life
1933	20	First performance of Sinfonietta. Wins Ernest Farrar composition prize again. First performance of three movements from unpublished, unfinished string quartet, *'Go play, boy, play'*. Passes ARCM examination. *A Boy was Born*.
1934	21	*Simple Symphony*, based on juvenilia composed between 1923 and 1926; Britten conducts first performance. Father dies at Lowestoft, while Britten is in Florence. *Te Deum* in C major. *Holiday Diary*.
1935–9		Earns living in London by writing incidental music for the theatre, documentary films and radio features.
1935	22	Meets W H Auden in July. Suite for violin and piano Op 6 and *Friday Afternoons* completed.
1936	23	Signs publishing contract with Boosey and Hawkes. Joins permanent staff of GPO Film Unit. Unpublished march, *Russian Funeral*, for brass and percussion, first performed at Westminster Theatre on 8 March, conducted by Alan Bush.
1937	24	His mother dies. And his friendship with Peter Pears begins. He acquires the Old Mill at Snape.
1938	25	His sister Beth marries. Performs Piano Concerto.
1939	26	Leaves UK with Pears and first goes to Canada and then to New York. *Les Illuminations*, Violin Concerto.
1940	27	Seriously ill at the beginning of the year. At the end of October he had finished the *Michelangelo Sonnets* dedicated to and composed for Peter Pears.
1941	28	Frank Bridge dies. *Paul Bunyan* is first performed at Columbia University.
1942	29	Return to the UK. As a Conscientious Objector he is exempted from military service.
1943	30	*Serenade* for tenor, horn and strings.
1945	32	First performance of *Peter Grimes* at Sadler's Wells, London. Visit to Belsen concentration camp with Yehudi Menuhin.
1946	33	*The Rape of Lucretia* is first performed at Glyndebourne and then taken on tour.

Year	History	Culture
1933	Nazi Party wins German elections. Adolf Hitler appointed chancellor. F D Roosevelt president in US.	Malraux, *La condition humaine.* Gertrude Stein, *The Autobiography of Alice B Toklas.* Invention of FM radio.
1934	In Germany, the Night of the Long Knives. In China, the Long March (until 1935).	Shostakovich, *Lady Macbeth of Mtsensk.* Deaths of Elgar, Delius and Holst. Fitzgerald, *Tender is the Night.* Henry Miller, *Tropic of Cancer.*
1935	In Germany, Nuremberg Laws enacted. Philippines becomes self-governing. Italy invades Ethiopia.	Gershwin, *Porgy and Bess.* Richard Strauss, *Die schweigsame Frau.* Isherwood, *Mr Norris Changes Trains.* Marx Brothers, *A Night at the Opera.* Death of Alban Berg.
1936	Germany occupies Rhineland. Edward VIII abdicates throne in Britain; George VI becomes king. Léon Blum forms 'Popular Front' government in France.	Prokofiev, *Peter and the Wolf.* A J Ayer, *Language, Truth and Logic.* BBC television inaugurated. Hindemith, *Trauermusik.*
1937	Arab-Jewish conflict in Palestine. Japan invades China. Nanjing massacre.	Sartre, *La Nausée.* Steinbeck, *Of Mice and Men.* Picasso, *Guernica.*
1938	In Soviet Union, trial of Nikolai Bukharin and other political leaders.	Elizabeth Bowen, *The Death of the Heart.* Graham Greene, *Brighton Rock.*
1939	Stalin and Hitler sign non-aggression pact. 1 September: Germany invades Poland. Second World War begins.	Steinbeck, *The Grapes of Wrath.* John Ford, *Stagecoach*
1940	Germany occupies France, Belgium, the Netherlands, Norway and Denmark. In France, Vichy government established. Britain retreat from Dunkirk.	Hemingway, *For Whom the Bell Tolls.* Chaplin, *The Great Dictator.* Disney, *Fantasia.*
1941	Operation Barbarossa: Germany invades Soviet Union. Italians expelled from Somalia, Ethiopia and Eritrea.	Brecht, *Mother Courage and her Children.* Orson Welles, *Citizen Kane.*
1942	Japanese take Kuala Lumpur, Rangoon, Singapore. Battle of Stalingrad. Battle of Midway. Battle of El Alamein.	Shostakovich, Symphony No 7 ('Leningrad').
1943	Siege of Leningrad ends. Mussolini overthrown. 7 September: Italy surrenders.	Rodgers and Hammerstein, *Oklahoma!.* T S Eliot, *Four Quartets.*
1945	Yalta Agreement. 9 May: Germany surrenders. United Nations formed. In Britain, Clement Attlee becomes PM.	Evelyn Waugh, *Brideshead Revisited.* Karl Popper, *The Open Society and its Enemies.*
1946	Cold War begins. Italian Republic formed.	Bertrand Russell, *History of Western Philosophy.*

Year	Age	Life
1947	34	English Opera Group is formed and gives the first performance of *Albert Herring* at Glyndebourne.
1948	35	First Aldeburgh Festival opens with a performance of *Saint Nicolas* at the Parish Church.
1949	36	The *Spring Symphony* receives its premiere at the Holland Festival. Autumn: North American recital tour with Pears.
1951	38	*Billy Budd* first performed at Covent Garden, Britten conducting.
1952	39	First television production of a Britten opera: *Billy Budd*.
1953	40	Gala performance of *Gloriana* at Covent Garden as part of the Coronation celebrations of Queen Elizabeth II.
1954	41	Premiere of *The Turn of the Screw* at the Teatro la Fenice, Venice.
1955	42	Concerts with Pears in Belgium and Switzerland. English Opera Group overseas tour of *The Turn of the Screw.* World tour.
1956	43	German tour with Pears.
1957	44	First performance of full-length ballet, *The Prince of the Pagodas*, at Covent Garden, Britten conducting. English Opera Group tour of Canada. Britten later visits Berlin and moves into the Red House, Aldeburgh.
1958	45	*Nocturne*. Publishes *The Story of Music* (co-author: Imogen Holst).
1960	47	Premiere of *A Midsummer Night's Dream* in reconstructed Jubilee Hall, Aldeburgh.
1961	48	First performance of Cello Sonata at Jubilee Hall, Aldeburgh, by Rostropovich and Britten.
1962	49	*War Requiem* is first performed at the rebuilt Coventry Cathedral.
1963	50	50th birthday celebrations: all-Britten Prom, new production of *Peter Grimes* at Sadler's Wells and *Gloriana* at the Royal Festival Hall
1964	51	First performance of Cello Symphony in Moscow, with Rostropovich as soloist and Britten conducting.

Year	History	Culture
1947	Puppet Communist states in Eastern Europe. India becomes independent. Chuck Yeager breaks the sound barrier.	Tennessee Williams, *A Streetcar named Desire.* Camus, *The Plague.* Genet, *The Maids.*
1948	Marshall Plan (until 1951). Berlin airlift. In Britain, welfare state created.	Brecht, *The Caucasian Chalk Circle.* Mailer, *The Naked and the Dead.*
1949	People's Republic of China created.	Orwell, *1984*
1951	ANZUS Pact in Pacific. In Britain, Churchill returns to premiership.	Stravinsky, *The Rake's Progress.* J D Salinger, *The Catcher in the Rye.* Death of Schoenberg.
1952	Gamal Abdel Nasser leads coup in Egypt. Elisabeth II becomes Queen.	Tippett, *The Midsummer Marriage.* Beckett, *Waiting for Godot.*
1953	Stalin dies on same day as Prokofiev. Egyptian Republic formed. Mau Mau rebellion in Kenya (until 1957).	Dylan Thomas, *Under Milk Wood.* Arthur Miller, *The Crucible.*
1954	Nasser becomes leader of Egypt. French surrender at Dien Bien Phu. Indo-China Armistice signed in Geneva.	Kingsley Amis, *Lucky Jim.* Golding, *Lord of the Flies.* JRR Tolkien, *The Lord of the Rings.*
1955	West Germany joins NATO. Warsaw Pact formed.	Nabokov, *Lolita.* Satyajit Ray, *Pather Panchali.*
1956	Twentieth Congress of Soviet Communist Party; Nikita Khrushchev denounces Stalin.	
1957	Treaty of Rome; EEC formed. Sputnik 1 launched. Ghana becomes independent.	Bernstein (music) and Sondheim (lyrics), *West Side Story.* Poulenc, *Dialogues des Carmélites.* Bergman, *The Seventh Seal.*
1958	Pope John XXIII elected.	Death of Vaughan Williams.
1960	U2 affair. Sharpeville Massacre in South Africa. Congo becomes independent.	Fellini, *La Dolce Vita.* Hitchcock, *Psycho.*
1961	Berlin Wall erected. Bay of Pigs invasion. Yuri Gagarin is first man in space.	The Rolling Stones are formed. Nureyev defects. Truffaut, *Jules et Jim.*
1962	Cuban missile crisis. Second Vatican Council (until 1965).	Solzhenitsyn, *One Day in the Life of Ivan Denisovich.*
1963	J F Kennedy assassinated; Martin Luther King leads march on Washington.	The Beatles, 'She Loves You' and 'I Want To Hold Your Hand'.
1964	Khrushchev ousted by Leonid Brezhnev. First race relations act in Britain. Civil Rights Act in US.	Larkin, *The Whitsun Weddings.* Kubrick, *Doctor Strangelove.*

Year	Age	Life
1965	52	Newly established music division of Faber & Faber publish *Nocturnal* and *Curlew River*.
1966	53	Premiere of *The Burning Fiery Furnace* in Orford Church. The English Opera Group then takes it on tour in the UK and overseas.
1967	54	The Maltings Concert Hall is opened by Queen Elizabeth II. The English Opera Group participates in Expo '67 at Montreal.
1968	55	Edinburgh International Festival: programmes built around Schubert and Britten. Britten and Pears participate as performers.
1969	56	BBC TV production of *Peter Grimes* at The Maltings. On the night of the opening of the 22nd Aldeburgh Festival the Maltings Concert Hall burns down.
1970	57	Queen Elizabeth II attends the opening concert of the rebuilt Maltings.
1971	58	First performance of *Who are these Children?* at The Maltings
1972	59	Records Schumann's *Scenes from Goethe's Faust* for Decca at The Maltings
1973	60	Operation to replace a defective heart valve and long recuperation.
1974	61	First performance of Third Cello Suite by Rostropovich at The Maltings.
1975	62	On 9 July Britten attends performance of new production of *Peter Grimes* at Covent Garden. This was his last appearance at the Royal Opera House. In November he travels to Venice for the last time.
1976	63	First performance in UK of *Paul Bunyan*, as a BBC radio production and in the summer on stage at The Maltings. In June he is created a life peer. First performance of *Phaedra* with Janet Baker as soloist. On 4 December Britten dies at the Red House, Aldeburgh.

Year	History	Culture
1965	Military coup in Indonesia. Indo-Pakistan War.	Orton, *Loot*. Pinter, *The Homecoming*.
1966	Indira Gandhi becomes prime minister of India. H F Verwoerd, prime minister of South Africa, is assassinated.	Graham Greene, *The Comedians*. Plath, *Ariel*. Stravinsky, *Requiem Canticles*.
1967	Six Day War. Biafra War (until 1970). First heart transplant.	The Beatles, *Sergeant Pepper's Lonely Hearts Club Band*. Stoppard, *Rosencrantz and Guildenstern are Dead*.
1968	Martin Luther King assassinated. Soviet Forces invade Czechoslovakia. In Vietnam, Tet offensive.	Kubrick, *2001: A Space Odyssey*. The Rolling Stones, *Beggar's Banquet*.
1969	Irish troubles begin. Nixon becomes US president. Sino-Soviet frontier war. First man on moon.	Kenneth Clark, *Civilization*. Puzo, *The Godfather*. Shostakovich, Symphony No 14
1970	Israel and Syria clash over Golan Heights. Northern Ireland riots.	Simon and Garfunkel, *Bridge Over Troubled Water*. Greer, *The Female Eunuch*.
1972	US/Soviet Union detente. SALT I signed.	Berio, *Concerto for Two Pianos*. Richard Adams, *Watership Down*.
1973	Yom Kippur War. Denmark, Ireland and Britain enter EC.	Completion of the Sydney Opera House.
1974	Watergate scandal; Richard Nixon forced to resign.	Solzhenitsyn is expelled from the Soviet Union.
1975	Franco dies; King Juan Carlos restored in Spain. Angola and Mozambique become independent. End of Vietnamese War. Khmer Rouge seize power in Cambodia. Civil War in Lebanon.	Boulez, *Rituel in memoriam Bruno Maderna*. Spielberg, *Jaws*. Death of Shostakovich.
1976	Chairman Mao Zedong dies. Soweto massacre.	Alex Haley, *Roots*.

Rediscovering the Young Britten

Two Pieces (1929), for Violin, Viola and Piano
Un poco Andante – Allegro con molto moto

While researching this book in the archives of the Britten-Pears Library at the Red House, David Matthews came upon an unknown trio by the 16-year-old composer.

The trio is scored for the unusual ensemble of violin, viola and piano. It joins a number of recently unearthed works including a concerto for the same two string instruments. However, it stands out by dint of both its originality and startling accomplishment. This is far from being the score of an immature composer. In both movements, Britten reconciles great formal rigour with playful inventiveness; the piece marries astonishing colouristic richness with extraordinary sleight of hand. For example, at one point in the second movement, *Allegro con molto moto*, Britten asks the piano to speed up, while the violin and viola are emphatically ordered to remain *non accelerando*, producing an effect akin to jazz 'swing'.

Two Pieces was premiered at St John's, Smith Square, London on 10 July 2003, by Peter Sheppard Skærved, Dov Scheindlin and Aaron Shorr, at the concert to launch this book.

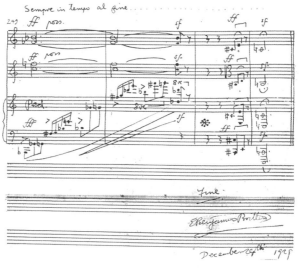

The closing bars of the second movement of *Two Pieces*: note the 16-year-old's strikingly mature hand

Works and Recordings

It is quite impossible to give a complete survey of Britten's output in a small study such as this. The full range of his vocal and editorial work, ranging from transcriptions of folk song and Schumann Lieder to his work on the music of Henry Purcell, is too extensive to include here. For a complete overview, see Paul Banks, *Benjamin Britten: A Catalogue of the Published Works* (Britten-Pears Library, 1999).

In the 20th century, no composer was more closely identified with the performance of his music than Benjamin Britten. No major composer before recorded such an authoritative cross-section of his *oeuvre*, resulting in an extraordinary catalogue of live and studio recordings. Not all of these can be guaranteed to be available at any one time, so, rather than recommending only those that are at the time of the publication of this book, below is a selection of the broadest possible range of available interpretations, primarily by the composer, or in the case of certain instrumental works, those by the dedicatee performers. Naturally, artists have continued to produce alternative versions of these works, and, in recent years, there has been considerable focus on the recording of his early works, but the authority of the composer's accounts is indisputable.

Operas

Paul Bunyan Op 17 1941

Peter Grimes Op 33 1945
Britten, Peter Pears, Claire Watson, James Pease, Owen Brannigan, Lauris Elms, David Kelly, Royal Opera House Chorus and Orchestra – *Decca* (1958)

The Rape of Lucretia Op 37 1946
Britten, Peter Pears, Heather Harper, Janet Baker, John Shirley-Quirk, Benjamin Luxon, Elizabeth Bainbridge, Jenny Hill, ECO – *Decca* (1970)

Albert Herring Op 39 1947
Britten, Sylvia Fisher, Johanna Peters, April Cantelo, John Noble, Edgar Evans, Owen Brannigan, Peter Pears etc, ECO – *Decca* (1964)

The Beggar's Opera Op 43 1948
(realized by Britten from the ballad opera by John Gay, 1728)

Billy Budd Op 50 1951
Britten, Peter Pears, Peter Glossop, Michael Langdon, John Shirley-Quirk, Bryan Drake, David Kelly, David Bowman, Robert Tear etc, Ambrosian Opera Chorus, LSO – *Decca* (1967)

Dido and Aeneas: Henry Purcell (realized and edited by Britten and Imogen Holst) 1951

Gloriana Op 53 1953

The Turn of the Screw Op 54 1954
Britten, Peter Pears, Jennifer Vyvyan, David Hemmings, Olive Dyer, Joan Cross, Arda Mandikian, English Opera Group Orchestra – *Decca* (1955)

Noye's Fludde Op 59 1958
Norman Del Mar, Owen Brannigan, Sheila Rex, David Pinto, Darien Angadi, Stephen Alexander, Trevor Anthony etc, East Suffolk Children's Orchestra, English Opera Group Orchestra – *Decca* (1961)

Operas (continued)

A Midsummer Night's Dream Op 64 1960
Britten, Alfred Deller, Elizabeth Harwood,
Stephen Terry, John Shirley-Quirk, Helen
Watts, Peter Pears etc, LSO – *Decca* (1966)

Curlew River Op 71 1964
Britten (musical supervision), Peter Pears,
John Shirley-Quirk, Bryan Drake, English
Opera Group – *Decca* (1965)

The Burning Fiery Furnace Op 77 1966
Britten (musical supervision), Peter Pears,
John Shirley-Quirk, Robert Tear, Stafford
Dean, English Opera Group – *Decca* (1967)

The Golden Vanity Op 78 1966
Britten (piano), Russell Burgess,
Wandsworth School Boys' Choir – *Decca*
(1969)

The Fairy Queen: Henry Purcell (realized
and edited by Britten and Imogen Holst)
1967

The Prodigal Son Op 81 1968
Britten (musical supervision), Peter Pears,
John Shirley-Quirk, Bryan Drake, Robert
Tear, English Opera Group – *Decca* (1969)

Owen Wingrave Op 85 1970
Britten, Benjamin Luxon, John Shirley-
Quirk, Heather Harper, Jennifer Vyvyan,
Janet Baker, Peter Pears, ECO – *Decca*
(1970)

Death in Venice Op 88 1973
Steuart Bedford, Peter Pears, John Shirley-
Quirk, James Bowman, ECO – *Decca*
(1974)

Ballets

Plymouth Town 1931

The Prince of the Pagodas Op 57 1956
Britten, Royal Opera House Orchestra –
Decca (1957)

Orchestral works

Two Portraits for Strings 1930

Sinfonietta Op 1 1932

Simple Symphony Op 4 1934
Britten, ECO – *Decca* (1968)

Soirées musicales Op 9 1936

Mont Juic Op 12 1937
Lennox Berkeley – *Lyrita* (1971)

Variations on a Theme of Frank Bridge Op 10
1937 Britten, ECO – *Decca* (1966)

Canadian Carnival Op 19 1939

Sinfonia da Requiem Op 20 1940
Britten, New Philharmonia Orchestra –
Decca (1964)

Paul Bunyan Overture 1941

An American Overture 1941

Matinées musicales Op 24 1941

Prelude and Fugue for 18 Solo Strings
Op 29 1943 Britten, ECO – *Decca* (1971)

Four Sea Interludes from *Peter Grimes*
Op 33a 1945

The Young Person's Guide to the Orchestra
Op 34 1945 Britten, LSO – *Decca* (1963)

Occasional Overture Op 38 1946

Chacony in G minor: Henry Purcell (arr
Britten) 1948

The Building of the House Overture Op 79
1967

*Suite on English Folksongs, 'A time there
was…'* Op 90 1974

Radio, film and theatre music (selection)

Night Mail 1936, *Love from a Stranger* 1936, *The Ascent of F6* 1936, *King Arthur* 1937, *On the Frontier* 1938, *Johnson over Jordan* 1939, *The Sword in the Stone* 1939, *The Rescue* 1943, *This Way to the Tomb* 1945, *The Dark Tower* 1945, *The Company of Heaven* 1937, *Men of Goodwill* 1947

Concertante works

Double Concerto for Violin, Viola and Orchestra 1932

Piano Concerto Op 13 1938
Britten, Sviatoslav Richter, ECO – *Decca* (1970)

Violin Concerto Op 15 1939
Britten, Mark Lubotsky, ECO – *Decca* (1970)

Young Apollo Op 16 1939

Diversions for Piano (left hand) and Orchestra Op 21 1940
Britten, Julius Katchen, LSO – *Decca* (1954)

Scottish Ballade for Two Pianos and Orchestra Op 26 1941

Movement for Clarinet and Orchestra 1942

Symphony for Cello and Orchestra Op 68 1963 Britten, Mstislav Rostropovich, Moscow Philharmonic Orchestra (live recording of premiere) *Russian Disc* (1964, rel 1993)

Lachrymae Op 48a for Viola and Strings 1976

Choral works with orchestra

Britten's output also includes numerous works for choir with instrumental ensemble or *a capella,* too numerous to include in this study.

Te Deum 1934

The Company of Heaven 1937

Pacifist March 1937

The World of the Spirit 1938

Ballad of Heroes Op 14 1939

Rejoice in the Lamb Op 30 1943
Britten, Michael Hartnett, Jonathan Steele, Philip Todd, Donald Francke, George Malcolm, Purcell Singers – *Decca* (1957)

Saint Nicolas Op 42 1948
Britten, Peter Pears, David Hemmings, Ralph Downes, Aldeburgh Festival Choir and Orchestra – *Decca* (1955)

Spring Symphony Op 44 1949
Britten, Jennifer Vyvyan, Norma Procter, Peter Pears, Royal Opera House Chorus and Orchestra – *Decca* (1960)

Cantata Academica, Op 62 1959
George Malcolm, Peter Pears, Helen Watts, Jennifer Vyvyan, Owen Brannigan, LSO and Chorus – *Decca* (1961)

Missa Brevis Op 63 1959

The National Anthem (arr Britten 1961)

War Requiem Op 66 1962
Britten, Galina Vishnevskaya, Peter Pears, Dietrich Fischer-Dieskau, David Willcocks, Simon Preston, Bach Choir, Highgate School Choir, LSO and Chorus, Melos Ensemble – *Decca* (1963)

Psalm 150 Op 67 1962
Britten, Boys of Downside School – *Decca* (1966)

Cantata Misericordium Op 69 1963

The Building of the House Op 79 1967

The Children's Crusade Op 82 1969
Britten, Wandsworth School Choir and
Orchestra – *Decca* (1969)

Welcome Ode Op 95 1976

Praise We Great Men 1976

Other choral works

A Boy was Born Op 3 1933
Britten, Michael Hartnett, Purcell Singers,
Boys of English Opera Group, Choir of All
Saints' Margaret Street – *Decca* (1957)

Friday Afternoons Op 7 1935
Britten, Downside School Choir, Viola
Tunnard – *Decca* (1966)

Hymn to St Cecilia Op 27 1942

A Ceremony of Carols Op 28 1942
Britten, Copenhagen Boys' Choir, Enid
Simon – *Decca* (1953)

Sacred and Profane Op 91 1975

Vocal works (selection)

Quatre chansons françaises 1928

Tit for Tat 1931
Britten, John Shirley-Quirk – *Decca* (1972)

Our Hunting Fathers Op 8 1936
Britten, Peter Pears, LSO – *BBC Enterprises*
(1966, rel 1981)

Les Illuminations Op 18 1939
Britten, Peter Pears, CBS Symphony
Orchestra – *NMC* (1941, rel 1995)

Seven Sonnets of Michelangelo Op 22 1940
Britten, Peter Pears (live) – *Melodiya*
(1966, rel 1985)

Serenade for Tenor, Horn and Strings Op 31
1943 Britten, Peter Pears, Dennis Brain,
Boyd Neel Orchestra – *Decca* (1944)

Now Sleeps the Crimson Petal, for Tenor,
Horn and Strings 1943

The Holy Sonnets of John Donne Op 35 1945
Britten, Peter Pears – *EMI* (1947)

A Charm of Lullabies Op 41 1947
Britten, Helen Watts – *BBC Enterprises*
(1963, rel 1981)

Canticle I, 'My Beloved is Mine' Op 40
1947 Britten, Peter Pears – *Decca* (1961)

Canticle II, 'Abraham and Isaac' Op 51
1952 Britten, Peter Pears, John Hahessy –
Decca (1961)

Winter Words Op 52 1953
Britten, Peter Pears (live) – *Melodiya*
(1963, rel 1985)

Canticle III, 'Still falls the rain – The
Raids 1940, Night and Dawn' Op 55
1954 Britten, Peter Pears, Dennis Brain
(live) – *IMG/BBC* (1956, rel 1999)

Songs from the Chinese Op 58 1957
Julian Bream, Peter Pears – *RCA* (1963)

Nocturne Op 60 1958
Britten, Peter Pears, LSO – *Decca* (1959)

Sechs Hölderlin-Fragmente Op 61 1958
Britten, Peter Pears – *Decca* (1961)

Songs and Proverbs of William Blake Op 74
1965 Britten, Dietrich Fischer-Dieskau –
Decca (1965)

The Poet's Echo Op 76 1965
Mstislav Rostropovich, Galina
Vishnevskaya – *Decca* (1968)

Who are these Children? Op 84 1969
Britten, Peter Pears – *Decca* (1972)

Canticle IV, 'Journey of the Magi' Op 86
1971 Britten, James Bowman, John
Shirley-Quirk – *Decca* (1972)

Canticle V, 'The Death of Saint Narcissus'
Op 89 1974 Osian Ellis, Peter Pears –
Decca (1976)

A Birthday Hansel Op 92 1975
Osian Ellis, Peter Pears – *Decca* (1976)

Phaedra Op 93 1975
Steuart Bedford, Janet Baker, ECO –
Decca (1977)

Instrumental and chamber works

Five Walztes for Solo Piano 1925

String Quartet in F 1928

Rhapsody for String Quartet 1929

Two Pieces for Violin, Viola and Piano
1929

Three Character Pieces for Piano 1930

Reflection for Viola and Piano 1930

Movement for Wind Sextet 1930

Quartettino for String Quartet 1930

Elegy for Solo Viola 1930

Twelve Variations for Solo Piano 1931

String Quartet in D major 1931

Sinfonietta Op 1 1932

Phantasy in F minor for String Quintet
1932

Phantasy Op 2 for Oboe, Violin, Viola and
Cello 1932

Alla Marcia, for String Quartet 1933

Holiday Diary Op 5 1934

Suite Op 6 for Violin and Piano 1935

Two Insect Pieces for Oboe and Piano 1935

Three Divertimenti for String Quartet 1936

Temporal Variations for Oboe and Piano
1936

Two Lullabies for Two Pianos 1936

Reveille, for Violin and Piano 1937

Introduction and Rondo alla Burlesca Op 23
no 1 1940
Britten, Clifford Curzon – *Decca* (1944)

Moderato and Nocturne from *Sonatina
Romantica* for Solo Piano 1940

Mazurka Elegiaca Op 23 no 2 1941
Britten, Clifford Curzon – *Decca* (1944)

String Quartet No 1 Op 25 1941

String Quartet No 2 Op 36 1945

Prelude and Fugue on a Theme of Vittoria for
Organ 1946

Lachrymae Op 48 for Viola and Piano 1950

Six Metamorphoses after Ovid Op 49 for Solo
Oboe 1951

Alpine Suite for Recorder Trio 1955

Sonata in C for Cello and Piano Op 65
1961 Britten, Mstislav Rostropovich –
Decca (1961)

Night Piece for Solo Piano 1963

Nocturnal after John Dowland Op 70 for
Guitar 1963

Suite No 1 for Solo Cello Op 72 1964
Mstislav Rostropovich – *Decca* (1968)

Gemini Variations Op 73 1965
Zoltán and Gábor Jeney – *Decca* (1965)

Suite No 2 for Solo Cello Op 80 1967
Mstislav Rostropovich – *Decca* (1968)

Suite for Harp Op 83 1969
Osian Ellis – *Decca* (1976)

Suite No 3 for Solo Cello Op 87 1971

String Quartet No 3 Op 94 1975
Amadeus Quartet – *Decca* (1978)

Tema 'Sacher' for Solo Cello 1976

Index

Europe, war in, 58
Evans, Nancy, 100
Expressionism, 10, 20, 78

Faber Music, 137
Fass, Marjorie, 23, 26, 46
Ferrier, Kathleen, 89, 107
Fischer-Dieskau, Dietrich, 131, 139
Fitzgerald, Edward, 97
Florence, 29
Ford, Ford Madox, 16
Forster, E M, 64, 97, 98; biography, 97; *Billy Budd*, 102–4, 106–7
Freud, Sigmund, 32, 37–8
Friston, 23

Gainsborough, Thomas, 102
gamelan music, 56, 79, 120, 121, 143
Gay, John, 95–6
German, Edward, 112
Gilbert and Sullivan, 92; *HMS Pinafore*, 106
Glyndebourne, 88, 93
Goodall, Reginald, 81
Goodman, Benny, 66
Goossens, Leon, 29
GPO Film Unit, 31
Graham, Colin, 125, 139
Grainger, Percy, 149
Grand Rapids, 52
Greatorex, Walter, 11–12, 14
Green, David, 37
Green, Kenneth, 81
Gresham's School, 11, 14, 41
Grierson, John, 31
Griller Quartet, 29
Group Theatre, 32, 88, 114
Guthrie, Tyrone, 95

Halifax, Nova Scotia, 67
Handel, Georg Frideric, 8, 92, 151; *Ode for St Cecilia's Day*, 141
Hardy, Thomas, 113
Harewood, Marion, 101, 106, 108, 116
Harper, Heather, 131
Hawkes, Ralph, 29, 51, 80, 137
Hely-Hutchinson, Victor, 28
Hemmings, David, 116–17
Henze, Hans Werner, 32, 60
Hesse, Peg, 116, 148, 154
Hesse, Prince Ludwig of, 116, 125
Hitler, Adolf, 45, 69

Hockey, Queenie, 2
Hockey, Willie, 2, 5
Hölderlin, Friedrich, 125
Hollywood, 62
Holst, Gustav, 8, 17, 98, 110; *Egdon Heath*, 150; *Planets*, 113; *St Paul's Suite*, 141
Holst, Imogen, 69, 82, 89, 101, 106, 107, 120, 154; assists Britten, 109, 110, 111, 116, 121, 138; in love with Britten, 109; biography, 110; conducts at opening of Maltings, 141; death, 156
Holt, 11
homosexuality, 32–3, 37–8, 39, 45, 70, 76, 97; law on, 42
Hopkins, Gerard Manley, 56
Horham, 144, 153
Hudson, Nellie, 124
Hugo, Victor, 10; *The Toilers of the Sea*, 13
Hussey, Revd Walter, 73

India, 119, 138
International Red Cross, 134
International Society for Contemporary Music (ISCM), 26, 29, 38, 45, 47
Ipswich, 2, 142
Ireland, John, 16, 17, 18, 24, 44; biography, 19
Isherwood, Christopher, 32, 33, 42, 43, 48, 75

James, Henry, 114–15, 142
Janáček, Leoš, 148
Jeney twins, 139
Jonson, Ben, 72
Jubilee Hall, Aldeburgh, 101

Kallman, Chester, 32, 56, 61, 126
Keats, John, 54, 73
Keller, Hans, 76, 106, 152; biography, 151
Khatchaturian, Aram Ilyich, 133
Kilvert, Francis, 108
Kirstein, Lincoln, 126
Kodály, Zoltán, 139
Koussevitzky, Serge, 80–81; Foundation, 67, 97

Lancing College, 41, 95
Lauricella, Remo, 23
Lawrence, D H, 32, 97
Layton, David, 14
Lee, Gypsy Rose, 61
Lemare, Iris, 23
London Labour Choral Union, 35
London Philharmonic Orchestra, 36

Picture Sources

The author and the publishers wish to express their thanks to the following sources of illustrative material and/or permission to reproduce it. They will make proper acknowledgements in future editions in the event that any omissions have occurred.

Richard Adeney p. 141; Doug Atfield p. 101; Alexander Bender p. 76; The Britten-Pears Library, Aldeburgh: pp. 2, 3, 4, 7, 12, 18, 31, 40, 46, 49, 54, 55, 57, 62, 63, 80, 89, 130, 134; East Anglian Daily Times p. 155; Roland Haupt p. iii, iv; Kurt Hutton pp. 94, 98, 111; Lotte Jacobi p. 60; Angus McBean pp. 79, 107; Planet News p. 84; George Rodger p. x; William Servaes p. 152; Brian Seed p. 122; Enid Slater p. 74; Clive Strutt p. 145; TopFoto pp. 90, 120, 132, 143, 157.